101 COOL WAYS TO MAKE MONEY

Written by Nicolas Brasch
Illustrations by Glen Singleton

HB
HINKLER
BOOKS

Published by Hinkler Books Pty Ltd

45–55 Fairchild St,

Heatherton Victoria 3202 Australia

www.hinklerbooks.com

© Hinkler Books Pty Ltd 2002, 2010

HB
HINKLER
BOOKS

First published in 2002 by Hinkler Books Pty Ltd

Written by Nicolas Brasch

Illustrated by Glen Singleton

Cover Illustration by Pete Beard

Edited by Rose Inserra

Page design by Chris Murphy

Page layout by DiZign

Printed & bound in China

978 1 7418 4293 7

★ Contents ★

Acknowledgments

Many thanks to all those kids and adults who provided much of the information, advice and tips contained in this book, including the staff and students of Fairfield Primary School, particularly Jenny Aitken, Sam Arwas, Eleonora Bertsa, Isabella Broman-Arrowsmith, James Crocaris, Bill Doring, Lachlan Gardiner, Kevin He, Lisa Hui, Rhys Kelly, Raffaele McQueenie, Erin Miller, Natasha Mpantellis, Alex Rooke, Bree Studd, Jessica Tweedale, Mike Wang, Letisha Watson, Darcy White and Alexia Yianoulatos.

Also special thanks to Oliver Astbury, Declan Buggle, Brigitte Douvos, Harry Glynn, Oliver Hutton, Sam Keogh, Emily O'Connor and Ashley Wannenburg—the entrepreneurs of the future.

Care to be Taken with Activities

A number of the activities in this book require special care to be taken. Please read the specific warnings below. We suggest you discuss these with your parents or a responsible adult when choosing to undertake an activity. They may even be able to help you decide the best way to approach the activity so you can make money sooner!!

Contact with Strangers

A number of activities involve contact with strangers. We all know that we have to be careful when talking to strangers, and this means being careful when we have business dealings with them too! Examples of these situations include selling goods door to door or going to the house of people you are not very familiar with to clean their pool, baby-sit their children or teach them computer skills.

It is important that you only do so if they are a friend, family member, have been recommended by a friend or family member, or you are accompanied by an adult you know well. You should always make sure that a parent or other family members know where you are, and you have discussed with them the suitability of the job for you. It may be that you need to be a bit older before visiting the house of people you do not know well. If this is the case, you could always do the job with an older friend or sibling—whilst this would mean sharing your earnings with them, you could get the job done in half the time, leaving more time to move on to the next job. Or more time to enjoy spending all the money you've earned!

Use of Dangerous Equipment

A number of activities in this book involve the use of potentially dangerous equipment such as chemicals, cleaning products, gardening tools, stoves, pools and ladders.

Care needs to be taken when using these products and equipment. They should only be used by children of the appropriate age and responsibility, and with parental or responsible adult guidance. Further, any products should only be used in accordance with the instructions and warnings provided by the manufacturer and supplier of that product.

Electrical Appliances

A number of activities suggested in this book involve working closely with electrical appliances. Examples of these are buying and selling second-hand goods, working with computers (such as cleaning and upgrading) and making electronic gadgets.

Extreme care needs to be taken when working with electrical appliances. This should only be done by people who have the proper knowledge and expertise, and if necessary, with adequate supervision.

Does the Activity Suit Your Age?

Some activities are better suited to certain age groups, so this is something you need to check before embarking on your new career. For example there is no point auditioning for the television commercial part of an eight-year-old if you are 14!—unless of course you are a very young looking 14-year-old! Likewise, some jobs will have a minimum age requirement such as stacking shelves at night or teaching swimming.

Other Things to Note

An important part of choosing an activity suitable to you is checking what that activity requires. Many activities have requirements specific to that activity. Examples of the requirements for certain activities include:

- making sure you have a permit for activities carried out on the street, such as busking or drawing caricatures
- making sure you tell customers the exact ingredients used in food you have prepared for sale—this is especially important if you make something containing nuts
- some activities will have business issues such as tax, insurance and registration requirements
- being careful not to breach copyright, for example by copying other people's designs for your web site or greeting cards
- checking whether you need your parent or guardian's permission for an activity, such as auditioning for a television show. However, whether or not their permission is needed you should always discuss your decision to choose an activity with a responsible adult before going ahead with the activity.

First Aid

It is always useful to have a first aid kit handy, or even to have done a first aid course. Having a certificate in first aid will also give you the edge over your competitors for many jobs, such as teaching swimming and babysitting.

Introduction

This book contains 101 cool ideas to make money. Some of them will be suitable for you, others won't. However, there is something in here for everyone—whatever your age, whatever your interests, whatever your talents, wherever you live.

Apart from the 101 cool ideas, there are chapters on 'Marketing Yourself', 'Setting a Price' and 'Web Site Resources'. Although many of the ideas have special marketing tips, you should still read the chapter on 'Marketing Yourself' because it gives good general advice on how you should market yourself. Good marketing can be the difference between a business succeeding or failing.

The 'Setting a Price' chapter explains how to set a price that both you and your customers are happy with. You want to make sure you earn a fair amount of money for the work you do but you can't charge too much or you won't get any customers.

The Internet is a great resource for information on jobs. However, like most subjects, finding the right information is not easy. In the chapter titled 'Web Site Resources' you'll find reviews for a few relevant web sites, as well as advice on how to use search engines to get the information you want.

COME AND GET IT! READ ALL ABOUT IT...! READ HOW TO MAKE SOME CASH!

101 COOL WAYS TO MAKE MONEY

Marketing Yourself

Marketing is an important part of any business. It involves making potential customers aware of the goods and services that a business has to offer. You could have the best product in the world but if people haven't heard about it, you won't make a cent. Nike and McDonald's may or may not have the best products on the market but the way that they have marketed themselves makes them the leaders in their field.

Tips

So how should you approach marketing? Exactly the same way as any business. Below are a few tips to help you. They are tips that all businesses should follow.

- Determine who your key market is. That means working out what types of people are most likely to want your goods and/or services. Are they male or female? What age group are they in? Are they individuals or businesses?

- Determine the best way to contact these people. Is it through advertising or personal contact? Should you produce printed material to put in mail boxes or go knocking on doors? Have you got contacts that can spread the word to your key market?

- Determine which of your qualities or which features of your goods and/or services are the best ones to market. If you are a happy-go-lucky person who makes a good personal impression, then sell yourself. If you have a product with a unique ingredient, focus on that ingredient.

- Know your competition. How do your competitors market themselves? What are they offering? What have you got to offer that they haven't?

Once you have answered the key questions, you will be in a great position to create a marketing campaign that will best suit you and your business.

Marketing Material

A marketing campaign often involves the production of marketing material. You should consider whether or not you need:

- flyers (a set of single page ads)
- posters
- business cards
- brochures
- signs
- a web site

101 COOL WAYS TO MAKE MONEY

More Tips

- The word 'Free' attracts attention, as do 'Two for One', 'Half-Price' and 'Today Only'.
- Offer discounts or bonuses to people who refer you to other customers. Word of mouth is the best marketing of all.
- Get feedback from customers. What do they like about your goods and/or services? What don't they like? The chances are that others will feel exactly the same way.
- Try and measure how successful different aspects of your marketing campaign are. Ask new customers how they heard about you. If you can determine which marketing works best for you—repeat it.

Good luck. And remember, 'The Customer is Always Right—Even When They're Wrong'.

Setting a Price

How much will I earn? What I can charge? Can I make a bit extra? These are the questions that most of you will be asking while you read the 101 cool ideas contained in this book. Unfortunately, the answers aren't simple. We have chosen not to include a guide to earnings for each idea because the amount you can earn will depend on so many different factors, including:

• your age
• your location
• your costs
• your customer's exact requirements
• your customer's ability to pay
• the speed at which you work
• your negotiating ability

However, some of the ideas do contain pricing information that may be relevant to that idea only.

Compromising

Basically, your customer will want to pay as little as possible, while you will want to charge as much as possible. Obviously, you won't both get exactly what you want. Therefore, most business is done at a compromise price, which is a price that both parties are satisfied with.

Some jobs are best suited to an hourly rate. However, if you take as long as you can so that you earn more, you may not get repeat business. Other jobs are best suited to a set fee. However, if you race through the work, you may not do a great job and, again, you won't be asked back. The best way to ensure you receive the most money over the long term is to forget about the money while you're actually working and concentrate on making sure that you do a great job.

The Benefits of Research

In order to set a price, you need to do some research first. Find out how much other people charge for the same item or service. If you're going to charge more than them, you're going to have to include something that the others don't offer. If you charge too little, potential customers may think that your product is no good or you're not going to provide a great service. You may find that you change your charges after a bit of experience.

Counting Your Costs

One of the most important things to do is make sure you make a *profit*. That means keeping track of how much you spend on all aspects of your business and then adding extra for your time. If a customer wants to bargain with you and offers less than the price you're charging, never agree to a price less than your costs. Otherwise you'll be out of business in no time.

Web Site Resources

The Internet is a great place to find information about ways to make money, how to market yourself and what particular jobs involve. Below are reviews of a few web sites you may find useful.

www.ehow.com

A site that contains instructions on how to do over 15,000 different things. They don't all have something to do with making money but those that do are very useful. You have to register to access the information but there is no cost involved.

www.kidsmoney.org

Tips, advice, articles and links on making money and what to do with the money that you've earned.

www.teachingkidsbusiness.com

Information on developing the right skills to help you succeed in the world of business.

www.kidslife.com

A site full of information sent in by kids, as well as links to other sites. Although it is not devoted to ways to make money, it does contain quite a few good ideas.

Using a Search Engine

If you have an idea that you want more information on, try searching for particular words and phrases in a web search engine. The best search engine to do this in is probably www.google.com.

If you receive too many responses to your request, keep typing in relevant words until you have reduced the list to a manageable number.

Making Money in Your Neighbourhood

Nº 1

Buying and Selling Second-Hand Goods

This is great fun for anyone who loves hunting through old boxes in attics and basements. Don't worry about the spider webs and the mould and the ghosts, just keep your head down. You don't want to miss out on anything. Virtually every item you find will be of some value.

OOOHHH...Boy! I was only a kid when this one was a hit!

OLD RECORDS

Finding Goods

To find goods you can sell, ask your parents, relatives and friends if there's anything they want to throw away or if they have boxes full of stuff that you can look through. Tell them you'll pay for any items you take. That'll get them interested.

Some of the most popular second-hand items are:

- books • bikes and skateboards • toys
- electrical items
- computer software
- clothes • CDs and records

MAKING MONEY IN YOUR NEIGHBOURHOOD

Finding Buyers

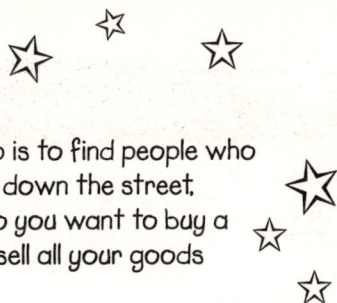

Once you've collected a few items, the next step is to find people who might want to buy them. You could always walk down the street, stopping everyone you meet and asking, 'Hey, do you want to buy a hamster cage?' However, it may take a while to sell all your goods this way. Here are some better suggestions.

This could be the start of my business empire!

SECOND HAND GOODS FOR SALE

BARGAINS!

BOOKS

RECORDS

Pull a cart full of goods around the neighbourhood (or attach it to the back of your bike). Ring a bell to draw attention to yourself or knock on a few doors along the way.

Set up a stall outside your house or along a busy section of your neighbourhood.

Rent a stall at a market.

Get you mum or dad or older brother or sister to take you to a car boot sale.

Setting a Price

You could try selling a second-hand Perry Como CD for a small fortune, but it's unlikely you'll get it. In fact, you could offer a second-hand Perry Como CD to someone for nothing and it's unlikely they'll take it. So it's important that you know the worth of the goods that you're buying and selling.

Basically, you want to sell an item for as much as you can. Obviously, it has to be at a price greater than you paid for it. If you have items that just won't sell, you'll have to reduce the original price you set. If a particular item is snapped up very quickly, make a note that the next time you have one of them, you should try to sell it for more.

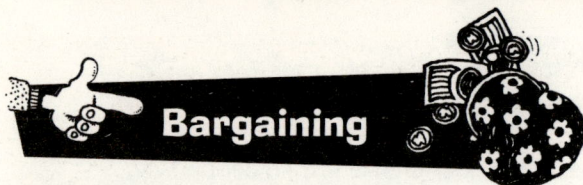

Bargaining

One of the most fun parts about buying and selling second-hand items is bargaining. Some people love bargaining, others hate it. However, if you're serious about making money from buying and selling second-hand goods, it's something you're going to have to do. When buying an item, offer less than you're willing to pay. When selling an item, price it at higher than you're willing to sell it for. This gives you room to bargain.

Special Tip...

You can increase the value of something you've bought by cleaning it, fixing it up, making it more attractive or adding to it. For example, add decorations or a bell to the handlebars of a bike. Just remember to include the cost of any additions when you're determining a price.

It's just what I've been searching for... a bike with absolutely EVERYTHING!

'You wouldn't believe what some people buy. I even sold a bag of rusty old screws and bolts.' —Jason

Nº 2

Raking Leaves and Shovelling Snow

These are jobs for particular seasons. You'll look pretty silly standing around with a rake in springtime or a shovel in the middle of summer. Mind you, you won't have much competition.

Normally these leaves wouldn't fall until autumn... ...but I have an enterprising mind!

The Great Outdoors

If you love working outdoors, then these jobs are for you. During autumn (fall), just walk around your neighbourhood, looking for gardens and pavements that are covered in leaves. You'll find plenty of them. Then ask if you can rake the leaves up. Don't forget to take lots of large garbage bags. You're going to have to take the leaves away and dispose of them. Ring your local council and find out the best place to get rid of the leaves. You never know, they may pick them up for you. If you live in a town where snow falls heavily in winter, then you may be able to shovel snow from people's driveways and pavements.

Nº 3

Gardening

Everyone can do something in the garden and get paid for it. Not only that, but you can enjoy the outdoors, listen to your Walkman and even bring your dog with you at the same time—and get paid for it!

Tasks

The type of jobs that have to be done depend greatly on the type of garden, the condition it is in and the season. But some of the things you may have to do include:

• pruning plants • trimming hedges • pulling out weeds • raking leaves • turning soil • planting seeds

👉 Equipment and Tools

You may be provided with garden tools but it's probably a good idea to provide your own. That way you look more professional and you won't miss out on doing jobs for people who can't provide you with garden tools. Basic tools you'll need are:

• **garden gloves** • **rake** • **secateurs**
• **trowel** • **fork**

👉 Special Tip...

Is there anyone in your neighbourhood who has a garden that hasn't been touched in years and which is full of junk? If so, offer to tidy up their garden for free. They'll think it's the offer of the century. Once they agree, tell them there's one condition attached—you get to keep anything that's lying among the overgrown grass, bushes and trees.

You never know what you'll find. And remember, there's always someone willing to buy old tools, toys and other objects.

WOH! Finders... keepers! Now whoever would have thought there'd be a bag of cash under this tiny tree

Must be a money tree!

'I learnt a very good lesson one day. Always have a first aid kit with you. I cut my hand while pruning some bushes and there was no-one in the house. I had to walk all the way home to fix it up.'—Alex

№ **4**

Mowing Lawns

Mowing lawns is a bit like cutting hair, only you're using much bigger scissors. Luckily you don't have to find a cape big enough to tie around the entire lawn! Actually, mowing lawns is one of those jobs that looks easier than it is. A bad mowing job stands out like a bad haircut.

What a lovely day it is today! Just look at that sky! Beautiful clouds.... ...a great day to mow!

How to Mow

Mowing lawns is far more than just pushing a lawn mower back and forward over a lawn. First, you have to make sure that the lawn is clear of stones, rocks and sticks. Otherwise, you could end up with a broken lawn mower that costs more to fix than you're trying to earn.

You also have to make sure that the edges are neatly trimmed. Sometimes the edges are too close to a wall or fence for the mower to reach, so you may need to use a special trimmer (or weed-eater) or even manual grass clippers, which are like giant scissors.

Then, of course, you have to dispose of the grass. Some of your customers may be happy for you top spread it on their garden, place it on a compost pile or in a bin to be collected with the garbage. However, others will want you to remove it completely.

Equipment and Tools

Some customers may have a mower that you can use, but you are going to get a lot more customers if you can supply your own mower. There are basically four types of mowers:

- **manual push mowers**
- **electric push mowers**
- **petrol push mowers**
- **petrol sit-down mowers**

When you mow the lower paddock... Please mow around the cows.... Mind you don't start a stampede!

Not the mower!

Manual push mowers are environmentally friendly but require a lot more work than the others. Although they are cheaper to buy, the length of time it takes to mow a lawn will reduce the number of lawns you can mow in a day and therefore affect your income. Electric push mowers are quieter than petrol mowers but you have to always beware of the power cord connected to the mower. Also, you can only mow someone's lawn when they are home, so that you are able to access a power point. Petrol push mowers are the most common type used and, though they make a fair bit of noise, do the job pretty effectively. Sit-down mowers are for the very lazy, those with a great deal of money (in which case, what are you working for?) or for those who need to mow a huge property.

So now you've got your mower sorted. You will now need:

- **a trimmer (weed-eater)** •**a grass blower** •**spare petrol**
- **a rake** •**manual grass clippers**

Transporting Your Mower

Now that you've got all this equipment, unless your customer lives next door or just around the corner from you, you're going to have to be able to transport the mower and the other equipment. You could ask Mum, Dad or an older brother or sister to drive you but then your availability to mow lawns is going to depend too much on others. How about building a trolley that can hold the equipment and be pulled along from job to job? You never know, someone might like your trolley so much that they'll pay you to build one for them. Maybe one day you could give up mowing lawns for building trolleys.

Special Tip...

- Always wear closed, strong shoes.
- Never try to fix or clean the mower blades while the mower is on.
- Keep your spare petrol can away from naked flames.
- Goggles will protect your eyes from flying stones and twigs.
- Wear a hat and sunscreen, even on a cloudy day.
- Use gloves when picking up clumps of grass. They'll protect you from hidden prickles and bugs.

Just hand me a mower! I'm ready to tackle any lawn!

Warning

You should only mow lawns of people you know or people who have been referred to you by friends and relatives. And always make sure that your parents know where you are going to be working.

> 'I always throw a bit of grass grower on the lawn when I've finished. It's great for business. Some lawns grow so fast I have to cut them every two weeks.'—James

Nº 5

Gift Wrapping

Oh bother...! I don't think I'll have quite enough paper for the stool !

Setting up a gift wrapping service in your neighbourhood is a good way to make pocket money from home. However, there will probably be times when you have little work and other times, such as Christmas, when you'll be so busy you might not even have time to go out and buy your own presents. To be a good gift wrapper, you have to be a creative and artistic person. No-one's going to use you again if your work pokes out everywhere and has sticky tape hanging off the edges.

How to Wrap

- When you cut the paper, make sure it is enough to cover the entire parcel and a little bit more.
- Lay the paper on the table, then place the parcel on top. Don't try to wrap the paper around the parcel.
- Make sure your folds are neat and tidy.
- The tighter the wrap, the better.
- Ribbons and bows can make all the difference.
- Practice makes perfect. Before you start wrapping for other people, wrap boxes and parcels of all shapes and sizes.

Marketing Tip...

Here's a good idea for getting work. Buy some tiny boxes, place a neat note advertising your services inside each one, then wrap them, put a decorative item on top and place them in letter boxes around your neighbourhood. If you've done a good job, business should quickly flow your way.

GIFT WRAPPING

DAD... what sort of effect do you think this will have on my prospective customers?

Equipment

•paper of all different colours, patterns and textures (the more choices your customers have, the better) •boxes of all shapes and sizes, in which to put the gifts •scissors •tape •an object, such as a ruler, that helps you fold the paper evenly and neatly •ribbons and bows •envelopes and cards (the more services and features you offer, the more you can charge) •decorative items, such as flowers and other plant life, to tie on top of the parcel

Nº **6**

Babysitting

> Mum said to remind you that the cold pizza, chocolate cake and drinks are not for the babysitter...!

Babysitters have to be reliable, responsible and vigilant. After all, you're looking after the most valuable thing in the world—someone's child or children. You can't spend the whole time talking to your friends on the phone or chatting on the Internet. That only happens on TV shows. However, there are some bonuses. You can usually help yourself to whatever's in the fridge.

Duties

A babysitter's duties depend on whether it's daytime or night-time. During the day, you'll have to feed the kid(s), play with them and keep them out of mischief. At night-time, you'll have to play with them, get them ready for bed and make sure they are fast asleep by the time their parents get home. The type of thing you do with the kids you're looking after depends on their age and their interests.

MAKING MONEY IN YOUR NEIGHBOURHOOD

A baby is not going to be able to play skipping games and a six-year-old is not going to be interested in colouring in a picture of a teddy bear. Nevertheless, here are some ideas on how you can keep most kids occupied:

- **read books to them**
- **paint pictures together**
- **put on a puppet show**
- **watch TV or videos**

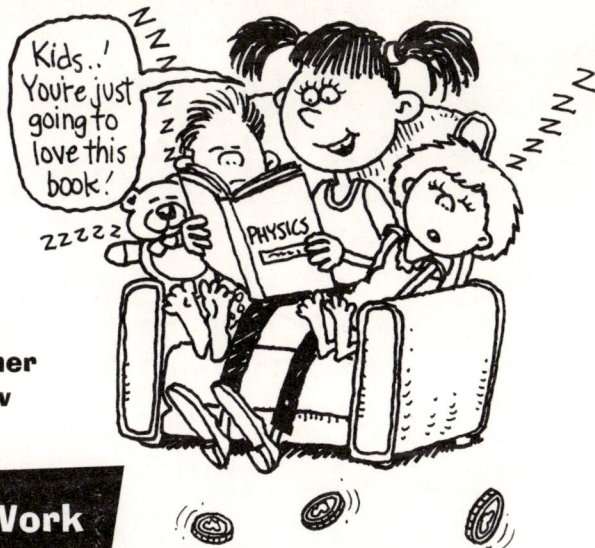

Getting Work

You can put flyers up in shop windows and other places in your neighbourhood but most parents will only use a babysitter they know or who has been recommended to them. Ask your parents to tell their friends that you're available. Once you've baby-sat for one family (and you haven't done any permanent damage to home or child), you'll find that word spreads quickly.

Special Tip...

- Learn CPR and first aid—you never know when you'll need it.
- Be punctual—remember, the people you're babysitting for are going out.
- Get a phone number for where the parents will be.
- Know the local emergency phone numbers.

Marketing Tip...

Why not suggest doing a few jobs around the house for some extra money? You could wash up some dishes, clean the house or even tutor the kid(s) you're babysitting.

Nº 7

Shopping for the Neighbours

I managed to find the last packet of genuine Transylvanian freeze dried bat wings in the entire supermarket!

There are many different reasons that people in your neighbourhood may want someone else to do their shopping for them. They may be elderly or sick; they may work long hours and not have time; they may just hate shopping. Whatever the reason, it represents an opportunity for you. Some people may want their shopping down regularly, others just from time to time. And then there are those people who are busy preparing for a dinner party and forgot an important ingredient for a dish they're making (such as the bat wings they need for a snail and bat stew). They'll give you a ring and you'll race out and find what they need.

MAKING MONEY IN YOUR NEIGHBOURHOOD

Setting a Price

You don't have to charge everyone the same rate. Someone who needs your services because they are working long hours at a high-powered job is able to pay more than someone on a pension who can't walk to the shops. Also, you can have a special 'emergency rate' for people wanting items in a hurry, such as a missing ingredient for a cake. What you do have to make sure is that you charge less than the shops charge for home delivery. Otherwise, you'll get very little business.

Special Tip...

If there are a few shops near where you live, try to do a deal with one of them. Promise to conduct your shopping business in their store, in return for a discount on their prices. Of course, you still charge your customers the full price. That means, you're really getting paid twice for the same job: once from your customer, for the shopping you're doing for them; and once from the shop, in the form of a discount.

Apples...
Apricots...
Artichokes...
Aluminium Foil

'I love shopping. It doesn't matter what I'm buying. I just adore it. So this is the perfect job. Doing someone else's shopping and getting paid for it.'–Natasha

101 COOL WAYS TO MAKE MONEY   27

№ 8

Reading Stories to Young Kids

If there's one thing that parents get sick of doing, it's reading the same stories to their children, over and over again. They'll pay any amount to have someone else take over this job. Well, maybe not any amount but enough to make it worth your while.

Read the page on DUMPTRUCKS again please!

Gee! Mum and Dad have never read this book on Earthmoving equipment to us before!

Just look at the tracks on that BULLDOZER!

👉 Proving Popular

This is a job that you could do after school. That's the time of day when mothers (or stay-at-home fathers) have just about had enough of their young children. It's also when the children start getting grumpy because they're tired. Now, if you offer to drop by after school and read a few books to a child, while their parent prepares dinner (or has a nap), you'll be the most popular kid in the neighbourhood. You might also be lucky enough to score some cookies or an ice-cream.

👉 Special Tip...

Once you know what type of books a child likes to have read to them, start borrowing appropriate books from the library for them. It shows the care you have for your job and for the child and word will soon spread throughout the neighbourhood.

👉 Special Warning

...and they all lived happily ever after... THE END

Hey! What about the story?

Be warned: young children remember every word in a book. Don't try to skip sentences of pages because you'll be caught out and probably have to go back to the beginning.

Nº **9**

Washing Cars

Put on your wetsuit, swimming costume or diving gear because this is a job where you're going to get very wet. Washing cars involves hosing a car with water, then scrubbing the outside with a sponge and detergent, rinsing the detergent off and wiping the windows so that there are no smear marks left on them. You may also wish to add extra services, such as applying special car wax to the outside and vacuuming the inside. After all, the more you can offer, the more you can charge.

Boy! You're obviously the sort of kid who takes his work pretty seriously!

Equipment

Whether you conduct your business from your home or you wash cars at your customers' houses, you're going to need the following equipment:

• hose • sponges • cloths • car washing detergent • car wax • vacuum cleaner (small battery operated car vacuums are available) • chamois (for drying, particularly the windows)

And, of course, you're going to need access to water, otherwise you're going to get a very sore tongue licking the car clean.

'I got a fair bit of business by putting my flyer under the windscreen of really dirty cars.'–Adrian

Special Cleaning Tips...

• Making sure all the windows are tightly closed. It's an obvious tip but it's amazing how many people forget to check the windows. Also check the sunroof.

It's bad enough that the water got in the car... But what I want to know is how the FISH got in the car!

• Don't spray the car too hard with water. If there's too much pressure, you might end up chipping paint off the surface.

• Don't use normal laundry detergent to wash the car. It can damage the surface.

Nº 10

Cleaning Houses

Cleaning houses is a very big business. That's because there are lots of people who are too busy or couldn't be bothered to clean their own house. That's the good news. The bad news is that there's a lot of competition out there.

Mum often says she wishes I could clean my room with the same speed and enthusiasm.... BUT THIS IS MY BUSINESS!

Tasks ☆ ☆ ☆

So what types of jobs are so many people avoiding while almost as many are virtually knocking down doors to do them? They include:

- **dusting surfaces** • **mopping floors** • **vacuuming carpets**
- **scrubbing showers** • **cleaning toilets** • **cleaning ovens**
- **washing windows**

The list goes on and on. Some of the householders may expect you to wash their dishes or hang clothes on the line. Others are so house proud that they don't even like their cleaner seeing the house in a dirty state. These people will actually give their house a bit of a clean before you turn up. But don't be misled into thinking they've done half your job. These people are the type who'll follow you around rubbing their fingers along surfaces to make sure you haven't missed anything.

Equipment

The type of equipment you'll need depends on what equipment your customers have. Between you and them, you'll probably need some or all of the following items:

- **vacuum cleaner** • **mop** • **broom** • **bucket** • **dusters** • **sponges**
- **rubber gloves** • **carpet cleaning solution** • **floor cleaning solution** • **all-purpose cleaning solution** • **oven cleaning solution**
- **window cleaning solution** • **furniture polish**

MAKING MONEY IN YOUR NEIGHBOURHOOD

Marketing Tip...

If you know of someone in your neighbourhood who is moving out of their rented house, offer to clean the house for them. In order to claim back the money they left as a bond against damage or unpaid rent, they have to make sure the house has been properly cleaned. Given that they have to pack up, move and then unpack at the other house, it's likely they'll be more than happy to pay someone to clean the house for them.

Special Cleaning Tips...

- Don't use too much polish on wooden furniture. A thorough rub with a cloth, dabbed with a tiny amount of polish, will bring the best out of the wood.

- Don't automatically wash or wipe wallpaper. Some wallpaper may react to water or particular cleaning solutions. The best way to test whether it is safe to clean a particular type of wallpaper is to clean a tiny part of it, preferably a part that is hidden from general view.

- Most oven cleaning solutions are dangerous. Follow the instructions exactly and avoid breathing the solution or allowing it to touch your skin.

Aunty Mary assured me that cleaning her house was just like tidying my room... Only Aunty Marys house is fifty times bigger than my room!

Warning

You should only clean houses of people you know or who have been referred to you by your friends or relatives. And always make sure that a parent or other family members know which house you are cleaning.

'I thought cleaning a house would be like cleaning my room. But it's not. My auntie offered me a job cleaning her house. After four hours I'd only done the kitchen and bathroom and was exhausted. In the end, my auntie had to help me finish and I went looking for another job.'–Freya

№11

Cleaning Swimming Pools

To clean a swimming pool, you have to get into a wetsuit and swim underwater scrubbing the side of the pool with a toothbrush.
Only joking! But swimming pools do attract a lot of bacteria that can cause illness so cleaning a swimming pool requires a lot of work and close attention.

I thought it would be better to drain the pool dry... to give it a really good scrub!

What to Clean

There are three main areas that have to be thoroughly cleaned to ensure a swimming pool is safe and clean to swim in. These are the surfaces (walls and floor), the water and the filter. There are some vacuum cleaners that will clean all surfaces and the water merely by plugging them in and flicking a switch. However, if a swimming pool owner has one of these, it's unlikely they'll need you.

How to Clean

So, assuming you don't have access to a super-dooper vacuum, here's what you have to do.

1. Surfaces have to be scrubbed with a brush, with all mould and algae thoroughly removed. Brushes can be attached to long poles so it is not necessary to actually enter the water.

2. Leaves and other debris have to be removed from the surface of the water. This is best done with a net attached to a pole.

3. The pool has to be vacuumed. Pool vacuum cleaners do most of the work themselves but it is important to make sure you follow the starting and operating instructions exactly.

4. You have to clean the filter. Again, each filter will have its own cleaning instructions that have to be followed exactly.

5. Chlorine and/or other solutions need to be put into the pool. Before pouring anything into the pool, make sure you discuss it with the pool's owner.

Equipment

A lot of pool owners will have their own cleaning equipment. You may choose to clean only for those people who have the equipment because buying the equipment will cost a lot of money. You'll need:

The chlorine was a little strong... but I was still enjoying myself in there...none the less

•a pool vacuum cleaner •a brush •a net •a pole (for extra length so that you can attach the net and brush to it) •cleaning solutions, including chlorine

Special Tip...

- When brushing surfaces to get rid of bacteria, make sure you don't ignore the steps and corners.
- When you have finished, sweep and mop the pool deck area. This will help stop dirt and bacteria being taken into the pool.

'On hot days, I always have a swim after I've cleaned a pool. If the owners say anything, I just tell them I'm checking that I got everything out.'—Toby

Warning

A leaf!!.....I'll get it!.... It's mine!

- You should only consider this job if you are an experienced swimmer. You may have to work unsupervised and you need to be able to save yourself if you fall in.

- As with any job at people's houses, only work for people you know or people who have been referred to you by friends or relatives.

- Follow the instructions on chemical containers exactly. The wrong chemical balance could cause injury to you or people using the pool.

Nº 12

Home Security During Holidays

MUM! Will I get my ten big brothers and their friends from the wrestling club ...and Rex the guard dog for dinner now?

Think I'll try someone else's place

Somewhere a little less ...crowded

Most burglaries occur during the holiday season. After all, that's when houses are most likely to be empty. You can help prevent crime and make a bit of money at the same time by looking after your neighbours' houses. This idea involves making it appear as though someone is home. Burglars are much less likely to strike if they think someone is home.

What to Do

- Turn lights on and off at irregular times.
- Turn water sprinklers on and off at irregular times.
- Turn the television set on in the evening (don't forget to turn it off later at night).

- Open and close blinds at the beginning and end of the day.
- Take the mail in.
- Put the garbage bin out.

And why not water the owners' plants while they're away, particularly pot plants left inside? Although this may not be part of your job, it could earn you a few extra dollars.

Marketing Tip...

Security firms use scare tactics to get business. You could try the same. Before approaching neighbours, get the latest crime statistics for your area from the local police station, then use these figures to convince your neighbours into hiring you.

There's just something I don't like about that guy... Maybe it was the way he picked up the TV while I was still watching it!

'Three houses in our street got robbed last Christmas holidays. I was minding our next door neighbour's house and it wasn't touched. They were so grateful they gave me twice as much money as we'd agreed on.'—Emily

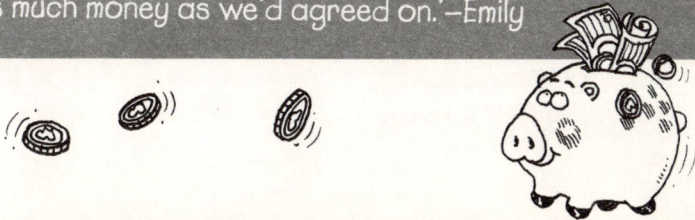

№ 13

Picking and Selling Fruit

Look around you. There are fruit trees everywhere. In every neighbourhood, lemon trees, apple trees, orange trees, plum trees and many other types of fruit trees are growing in people's backyards. Although much of the fruit ends up being used, much of it also goes to waste. After all, there are just so many apple pies one family can eat.

Finding Suppliers

So, why not go around the neighbourhood, asking if people have fruit trees in their gardens? If they do, offer to buy the fruit from them. You can also ask about vegetables, particularly tomatoes that grow like mad.

Once you've found your suppliers, you're probably going to have to pick the fruit off the trees yourself. For this you'll need a ladder, as well as a pole with a net or other catching device attached to the end. Remember to pick the fruit just as it's turning ripe. Most fruit continues to ripen even after being picked, so it need not be at its ripest when you pick it.

I thought I'd have an edge on the opposition having a monkey as a business partner. But there's just too much monkeying around!

MAKING MONEY IN YOUR NEIGHBOURHOOD

Selling the Fruit

Once you've got a decent supply of fruit, you can set up a stall or try selling it door to door. Remember, make sure you sell the fruit for more than you bought it for. You never know, one day you might end up running a chain of fruit shops.

Special Tip...

Be very careful to check that the branches of the fruit trees you're about to climb are not touching power lines. If a branch comes into contact with electricity, the whole tree may become electrically charged.

Pricing Tip...

As most people buy their fruit from the local fruit shop or supermarket, make sure you've got a competitive advantage by pricing your items lower than the shops. Before setting out with your goods, visit the local stores and check that day's prices. Fruit and vegetable prices can change daily.

BARGAIN! As many COCONUTS as you can carry away for the price of one in the shops...!

№ 14

Helping out at Kids' Parties

There's nothing that young kids like more than a party. And there's nothing that parents dread more than a kid's party. There's so much to prepare beforehand, so much work involved in making sure it runs smoothly and so much work involved in cleaning up. So the more you can help, the more grateful the parents will be (and the more money you can earn).

Oh thanks! I'd love what feels like 'A 1000 PIECE JIGSAW PUZZLE' ... but it's not my Birthday!

It's hers! I'm just working here...!

Before the Party

- Blow up balloons.
- Prepare food and drink.
- Set and decorate the table.
- Decorate the house and garden.
- Plan the games and activities.
- Set up the games and activities.

38

During the Party

- Take presents from the guests as they arrive.
- Serve food and drink.
- Lead the games and activities.
- Make sure every child is equally involved.
- Stop arguments.
- Bring out the host's presents.
- Take note of which present came from which guest.
- Hand out going home gifts.

After the Party

- Tidy up the mess.
- Wash up dishes.
- Pack away furniture and any props used for games.

Charging

> 'I learnt some magic so that I could dress up as a magician and perform some tricks. The parents would pay me extra because it meant they didn't have to hire a clown or magician.'–Barbara

The best way to charge for your work at a kid's party is on an hourly basis. Negotiate a price before you start. Make sure you charge more than for normal babysitting because you're going to be in control of many kids. Also, take advantage of the fact that parents will pay almost anything to have you take the stress away from them.

Special Tip...

Face painting is a great way to start off a kid's party. Animal faces are particularly popular and will have the kids running around enjoying themselves from the outset.

I'd like my face painted in the style of a 1500 lb Asiatic Black Bear from the northern foothills of the Himalayas chewing on berries and roots please!

You can do that can't you?

Helping out at Adults' Parties

I've gotta say... you've got me there! I don't know what it is... But it sure looks awful! I think it's black fish eggs!

This job is only for those at least 16-years-old. It's also the sort of job where you need another person working with you. If you're happy with these two conditions, read on. There's not much difference between helping out at a kid's party or helping out at a parent's party. After all, adults pretty much behave like kids when they have a party.

Before the Party

- Set and decorate the table.
- Set up a bar.
- Help prepare food.
- Set up a cloakroom.

MAKING MONEY IN YOUR NEIGHBOURHOOD

During the Party

- Take coats, jackets, hats and handbags from the guests as they arrive.
- Serve drinks on arrival.
- Serve food and drink.
- Clear away dirty glasses and dirty plates.
- Empty ashtrays.
- Hand back coats, jackets, hats and handbags to the right guests as they leave.

After the Party

- Tidy up the mess.
- Wash up dishes and glasses.
- Put clean dishes and glasses back in the right place.

Special Tip...

If the party is at night, organise how you're going to get home before the party starts. Arrange for one of the hosts to take you home or one of your parents to come and pick you up. You don't want to have to find your own way home in the dark.

Son! I hope you realise there's a surcharge involved for picking you up after 11.00 pm. How much pocket money have you got on you?

'I always charge a higher rate for working after 11.00 at night. I've never had anyone complain about it so I guess it's expected.'–Nicholas

№ **16**

Putting on an Art Exhibition

Oh dear! What a mess!

I know! Isn't it great! Want to buy it?

MY MESS

Art collectors sometimes pay an enormous price for a work of art. That's not to say that you could make that much (unless your surname is Picasso) but putting on an art exhibition can be a lot of fun. It also requires a lot of work, which is why it is probably best if you get a few friends together and share the tasks.

Collecting the Art Work

You can collect art work done by your friends and family or you can track down local artists and ask if they'd like to have some of their works included in the exhibition. It's probably best to have a combination of the two. Make sure that you take careful note of who supplied what, because you're eventually going to have to pay them or return their art.

MAKING MONEY IN YOUR NEIGHBOURHOOD

Finding a Venue

You need to book a hall or a large room that is suitable for exhibiting art. That means it has to have plenty of light and lots of wall space. The owners also have to be happy about you hanging up the art on their walls. The first place to try would be your local school. They may be happy for you to use a classroom, a gym or the hall, providing there will be a parent or even a teacher present throughout the exhibition.

Putting Up the Art Work

Here are some tips for hanging up paintings:

- Light the paintings with indirect lighting (i.e. not direct sunlight).
- Allow some space between the painting and the wall to allow for air to flow through.
- Don't hang paintings above heaters or air conditioners.
- Make sure the picture and hanging materials are well secured.

Putting Together a Catalogue

Prepare a catalogue with information about each painting. This information should include a photo of the art work, its title, details about the artist and the work's selling price. Then have enough copies of the catalogue printed so that you can hand one out to everyone who attends your exhibition.

Mock-up of a page from a catalogue:

Bowl of fruit, 2002
45 cm (18 in) x 30 cm (12 in)
Water colour on canvas
Stephen Lewis
Stephen is a full-time teacher and part-time artist. He has exhibited at several exhibitions and won a silver medal at the Springfield Art Show, 2000.

$80 (£30)

BOWL OF FRUIT 2002
45cm (18in) x 30cm (12in)
Watercolour on Canvas

$80 (£30)

SELF PORTRAIT 2002
60cm (24in) x 45cm (18in)
Oil on linen
$50 (£18)
2001

Self Portrait, 2002
60 cm (24 in) x 45 cm (18 in)
Oil on linen
Maggie Stewart
Maggie is an art student at Springfield Art College. She was Dux of Year 2001.

$50 (£18)

MAKING MONEY IN YOUR NEIGHBOURHOOD

Determining How to Make Money

There are two ways to make money at an art exhibition.

1 Through commission. That means that you receive a certain proportion of the sale price for each work sold. It's not unreasonable to ask the artists to give you up to 25% of the sale price in return for having their work displayed at your exhibition.

2 You can charge an admission price for entry to the exhibition. You have to be aware that if you do this, you are unlikely to get as many visitors as you would if admission was free. Ideally, you would have a small admission charge, as well as a commission arrangement with the artists.

Advertising

There's no use putting on an exhibition that no-one knows about. You have to advertise. The best way to do this is to design and print some flyers and posters and distribute them to your family members and around your neighbourhood and school. Make sure there's a picture of one of the best works of art on the flyer and poster but ask the artist's permission first.

Returning Unsold Paintings and Distributing Money

Once the exhibition is over, you have to return the unsold art work to the artists and deliver payment to those artists whose work was sold. Do this right away because it will make them more likely to participate in your next exhibition—that is if you haven't been scared off by the experience.

Special Tip...

When someone buys a picture, do not take it down and give it to them straight away. Otherwise, you may end up with a half-empty room midway through the exhibition. Instead, put a red round sticker on the painting to indicate it has been sold and arrange for the buyer to come back when the exhibition closes to pick up their picture.

Stick the biggest sold sticker you've got on it my girl. I want everyone to know... IT'S MINE!

SOLD

Nº 17

Delivering Junk Mail

People who produce and deliver junk mail don't tend to refer to it by that name. For them, it's not junk. It's the opportunity to promote products and services or a chance to make a bit of pocket money.
But we'll call it junk mail because that's the way most people refer to it.

PIZZA

Check the mailbox after I'm long gone! You'll find a voucher for six free cans of DOG FOOD with every family size pizza and Garlic Bread

VURRRRRR

How to Get Business

1 Find the name of a company that specialises in distributing some material and then contact them. They will put you in touch with the person who coordinates distribution in your area.

2 Speak to local businesses and let them know that you're available to deliver marketing material for them.

Getting Paid

Most junk mail deliverers are paid a certain amount per hundred items they deliver. That means that the faster you work, the more you'll earn. But beware of two things. First, checks are made to make sure that all junk mail is delivered. So don't dump them in a bin and tell your coordinator that you've delivered them. You'll find yourself out of work very quickly. And beware of dogs. Don't take risks. It's not worth getting bitten just to deliver the menu of the local pizza shop.

'If it's a really hot day, I do my deliveries first thing in the morning or late in the afternoon. It's less draining and I earn my money quicker.'—Declan.

Nº 18

Garage Sales/ Car Boot Sales

A garage sale is not a sale of new and used garages (though that's an idea worth considering). It involves the sale of second-hand goods from someone's garage or front yard. That's where the name garage sale comes from. If you have a lot of stuff you no longer need, it's a great way to clear some room and make a bit of money. Get your family and friends to contribute as well. The bigger the sale, the more people you're likely to attract.

In some places where no-one is familiar with garage sales, you can have a car boot sale instead. This means that you fill up the boot (trunk) of your parents' car, get your parents to drive you to a local place and then you can sell your old stuff. You may need a permit from the council.

MAKING MONEY IN YOUR NEIGHBOURHOOD

Organising the Goods

There are two ways to organise the rubbish, I mean second-hand goods, that you want to sell. You can either arrange it in piles according to who is selling it, or you can arrange it by category (e.g. all the videos together, all the books together, all the furniture together etc). If you do it by category, it's harder to take note of who is owed money, though it's easier for the customers.

To make things easy, you can always come to an arrangement that the money will be shared equally at the end of the day, though that requires everyone contributing the same amount of goods.

Marketing

Flyers, posters, word of mouth and an advertisement in the local paper should ensure customers turn up. If there's a group of you organising a garage sale together, make sure it's held at the house that is on the busiest street.

Early Morning Warning

I got up so early to pick up bargains at your garage sale... I missed breakfast. I'll offer you top money for a bite of that toast!

There are some people who spend every weekend going to garage sales and try to buy the best items before anyone else arrives. These people don't take a lot of notice of the advertised opening time. So if you're holding a garage sale, don't be surprised if someone knocks on your door at 7.00 in the morning wanting to see the goods.

'The best part of a garage sale is the bargaining. People expect it. When I price the items, I always put a price a little more than I want because people always try to bargain you down.'—Shane

101 COOL WAYS TO MAKE MONEY

47

No 19

Stencilling House Numbers

Isn't it frustrating when you're looking for a particular house but few houses in the street have visible house numbers? Well, it's not just frustrating, it's also a great opportunity. Old gangster movies talk about the 'numbers racket'. Well, you can run your own numbers racket, and it's totally legal. Target those houses in your neighbourhood that have house numbers that are hard to see. Remember not to approach anyone you don't know, unless you have an adult with you.

Stencilling

Stencilling house numbers involves painting house numbers onto the kerb outside people's houses. To do this you are going to need:

•stencils •cloths •paint •a roller and/or brushes

The stencils should be made from cardboard or acetate (see instructions below on making stencils). The best paint to use on concrete is an acrylic based paint.

To paint a house number, follow these steps:

- Clean the area that you are about to paint. Make sure dust and dirt are removed.
- Place the stencil on the area.
- Apply paint to the roller or brush and paint the hole in the middle of the stencil.
- Lift the stencil up and use a small brush to apply paint if there are areas that need a touch up.

Making Stencils

You are going to need nine stencils, one for each number from 0 to 9. Making a stencil involves the following steps:

- Find numbers that are designed in a pattern that is clean, bold and decorative. The numbers should be about 10 centimetres (4 inches) high.
- Trace the outline of the numbers onto tracing paper.
- Place the tracing paper over cardboard or acetate that is at least 7.5 centimetres (3 inches) larger than the number on every side.
- Using scissors or a craft knife, cut the cardboard or acetate on the outline of the number.
- Remove any rough edges on the inside of the number.

More than Stencilling

You need not limit yourself to stencilling kerbs. You can also offer to stencil numbers onto letter boxes, front doors or posts. The best paint to use on wood is a flat exterior acrylic paint. You can also carry around samples of numbers to be screwed or glued to a surface.

Marketing Tip...

If you are trying to talk someone into letting you stencil their house number, tell them how important it is that the emergency services, such as fire, police and ambulances, be able to quickly identify their house.

Special Tip...

Before starting a number stencilling business, check with your council if you have to get permission from someone. There may be regulations on the size and colours of the numbers. You may also have to ask permission from the people in the houses on either side of your customer.

'I checked the window of the local real estate agent to see which houses were being sold. If I knew the person selling the house, I approached them and told them how great it would look if they had new numbers on the front of their house. It's amazing how many times that worked.'–Michael

Nº 20
Setting up Lemonade Stands

On hot days, there's nothing more refreshing than a cool glass of fresh lemon juice. In the United States, lemonade stands have been a very popular way for kids to make pocket money for many years. However, for some reason they've never been quite as popular in other countries, which is ridiculous. In Australia, for instance, the climate is perfect for selling cool drinks.

Picking a Location

To set up a soft drink stall, you need to find a popular location to put your table or home-made display. The best place is near a shopping centre or where lots of people or cars are passing. If you are setting up in a public spot, make sure you have permission from the council. If you are setting up outside a business or home, make sure you have permission from the manager or owner. You are also going to have to advertise your presence.

You can do this by putting up signs and posters but the best way to advertise yourself is to shout out loud.

Attract people walking or driving past by shouting out, 'Lemonade for sale' or 'Buy your nice cool juice here'. Don't be shy. Shy people won't make nearly as much money as loud people.

Recipe

This recipe is for lemon juice. Practise making a few and get feedback from your friends as to which they like best. Lemon juice should be tangy but not too strong. It should be sweet enough to be pleasant but not enough to be sickly. This recipe gives general instructions, rather than exact amounts because the amount of each item you use depends on personal taste, as well as the flavour and amount of juice in each lemon.

WOH! That's sour! I prefer the term TANGY better... I'll stir in some more sugar!

Ingredients:

- lemons • sugar
- water • ice

Method:

Squeeze the juice from six or seven lemons into a jug. Add one cup of sugar and start filling with water. Stir the mixture as you pour the water in and from time to time stop what you're doing and have a small taste. When you've got the flavour just right, add some ice cubes to the mixture to keep it cool, or store in the fridge until you need it. When serving the juice, add some mint leaves into the cup for extra flavour.

Special Tip...

You might think that soft drink stalls are only for warm days. And you'd be right. But on cold days, try selling soup. A cup of hot soup and a slice of crusty bread can be a very popular item in winter.

MAKING MONEY IN YOUR NEIGHBOURHOOD

 **Warning**

Use only fresh ingredients and if a jug of soft drink has been sitting outside for too long, tip out the contents and replace them. Customers want fresh, healthy drinks.

> Hmmm! Sounds like an interesting deal

LEMONADE THIS-A-WAY →
with free biscuits
free fries... radio playing
comfy chairs...
pleasant sales staff!

'Half an hour after setting up my drink stand, someone else did the same thing just down the road. We were both selling about the same number of cups until I had the idea of buying a packet of biscuits and offering a free biscuit with each cup. Suddenly, I was gaining most of the business.'
–Charlotte

Setting up a Cake Stall

CAKES

I was just driving by when this attractive cream cake caught my eye

The same rules that apply for a soft drink stand also apply to a cake stall. You have to set up in the right location, attract passers-by and make a product that people want.

Which Cakes to Sell

There are thousands of different cake recipes you can follow but some will be more complicated than others. Stick to the more simple recipes. They'll take less time to make (giving you more time to sell) and are more likely to turn out right.

Try different cakes to start with but take note of which ones sell best. Once you've run a cake stall a few times, you'll know which cakes are most popular and can concentrate on them.

Grown-ups generally like different types of cakes to children. Children go for cup cakes with sprinkles on top, while grown-ups will prefer a slice of orange or carrot cake. So which market should you aim for? Both. Have a selection of cakes to suit all age groups. That way, you'll have something to sell to each member of a passing family.

MAKING MONEY IN YOUR NEIGHBOURHOOD

Recipe

To get you started, here's a recipe for an apple cake.

Ingredients:

- 2 cooking apples, peeled and diced
- 1 cup sugar
- $1\frac{1}{2}$ cups plain flour
- 1 teaspoon bicarbonate of soda
- 1 teaspoon cinnamon
- 1 teaspoon mixed spice
- 1 cup broken pecan nuts
- 1 egg
- 125 grams (4.5 oz) butter

Method:

Melt the butter and then let it cool. In one bowl, sift the flour, bicarbonate of soda, cinnamon and mixed spice, then add the pecan nuts. Stir it up so that all the ingredients are mixed together. In another bowl, mix the pieces of apple with the sugar. Pour the cooled butter into a large mixing bowl and whisk an egg into it. Then add the apple and sugar mixture, followed by the ingredients in the other bowl. Mix it all together, then pour it into a greased 20 centimetre (8 inch) cake tin. Bake for 45-55 minutes at 180° Celsius (350° Fahrenheit).

Warning

Use only fresh ingredients. Customers want fresh, healthy cakes.

Special Tip...

You should have a list of ingredients next to each cake so that people can check what has been used in making them. Some people react badly to certain ingredients and by having a list it shows that you care for your customers.

That's an interesting taste! What did you put in these cakes?

PRUNES...See... it's listed here right on the side of the pack

№ 22

Selling Flowers

I can see a career in Floristry blossoming here! The right flowers... the right day and the right location!

ANY FRESHER... AND THEY'D STILL BE GROWING IN THE GARDEN!

FRESH PICKED **FLOWERS**

Pick your flowers, pick your day and pick your location. Get those three things right and you'll be well on your way to a career as a florist.

Picking Your Flowers

Picking your flowers means selecting the right flowers and picking them at their peak. Once they've been picked, they don't last long so don't pick flowers until you have enough to make an impressive display. Nothing looks worse than a flower seller with a couple of wilting daffodils and a small posy of cornflowers. The chances are they'll still be for sale at the end of a very long day. Flowers are best picked when they have tight buds and shiny leaves. Once you've picked the flowers, sort them into bunches, tie an elastic band around each bunch and wrap them in clear cellophane paper. Then place the flowers in buckets with a small amount of water in the bottom.

Picking Your Day

Picking your day refers to the day you choose to sell your flowers. No flower seller would dare to miss making sales on Mother's Day or Valentine's Day. These two days can account for a large part of a flower seller's total business.

Obviously, Saturdays and Sundays are better selling days than weekdays because people have more time for shopping and browsing. However, if you are going to set up a flower stall on a weekday, it's best to do so in the evening, rather than the morning because people are more likely to buy flowers on the way home than on the way to work.

Picking Your Location

Picking your location means selecting the best place from where to sell your flowers. There's no point setting up a stall in your front garden if you live in an isolated place where one person walks past every three weeks. The flowers will be in a pretty poor state before you sell them. In this case, ask a friend who has a front garden that many people walk past if you can set up your stall at their place. Other great locations are near a train station, close to a shopping centre or outside a hospital. However, you may need a permit from the local council to set up a stall in public areas such as these.

Ensuring a Supply

If you rely on picking flowers from your garden or from those of your friends, you'll probably run out of flowers quickly. In order to ensure you have a regular supply of flowers, all year round, find out where your local wholesale flower market is. The flower sellers at these markets sell mainly to florists and other businesses but many of them also sell directly to members of the public. If there's a farm nearby that grows flowers, offer to buy flowers directly from the farmer.

'The first time I sold flowers, they all died within a few hours. The same thing happened the second and third times. I finally realised what the problem was. I had the flowers out under a hot sun. The next day, I bought a large beach umbrella to provide shade. Now the flowers can last for days.' –Judy

Marketing Tip...

Offer special gift wrapping as an extra service for a small fee. You'll please your customers and earn a little more money. All you'll need is a supply of coloured tissue paper and ribbon, a pair of scissors and some sticky tape.

There! Look at that! I can see this gift wrapping service really boosting my sales!

Nº 23

Selling Christmas Trees

Yo...Ho...Ho...
Just water
these little
babies
and they'll
be huge
by
Christmas

BUY IN APRIL and SAVE HEAPS!

This is truly a seasonal idea. You won't make much money trying to sell Christmas trees in April. In fact you'll look pretty stupid. But in December, it's a great way to make money.

Getting the Trees

The first thing you're going to need to get this business off the ground is access to a pine plantation that grows some of its trees specifically for Christmas. Don't wait to the last minute before approaching them; contact them in the middle of the year. You may have to place an order this early.

Transporting the Trees

Once you've got your supply organised, you're going to have to organise transport. At the very least, you'll need a four-wheel drive or station wagon (and, of course, someone to drive it for you). Depending on how many trees you have ordered, you may need to make several trips.

Selling Your Trees

Let's assume that you placed your order, have picked up the trees and now have 20 Christmas trees stacked up in your back garden. You've got to get rid of them quickly or you'll have 20 dead Christmas tress that you need to dispose of. So put up signs around your neighbourhood, announcing 'Christmas Trees for Sale' and add your address and phone number.

Special Tip...

Some people are very fussy when it comes to selecting a Christmas tree. If your supplier offers you small ones or slightly damaged ones at a cheaper price, don't take them. You probably won't be able to sell them. Make sure any trees you get are at least 1.8 metres (5.9 feet) tall and have a neat triangular shape.

Could I interest you in some of our handmade decorative baubles to hang on your home delivered tree?

Marketing Tip...

You'll sell more Christmas trees if you are able to offer a delivery service. For this service, you can charge a little more money. Also, have some boxes of decorations on display and for sale. You may sell a few of these as well.

Making Money at Home

Nº 24

Shopping

You couldn't do those LAMB CHOPS for half that price could you..? I've got some big plans for the change out of this money!

This job involves making a trip to the local shopping centre when your family has run out of something and having an arrangement with your parents that you get to keep the change. Sometimes you'll earn more than at other times but it's an easy way to earn a bit of extra pocket money. If you live near a shopping centre or shopping strip that has a lot of grocery shops and supermarkets, you can shop around for the cheapest price for the items you have to buy. That way there'll be even more change left over.

Special Tip...

If your parents get smart and try giving you change that doesn't cover the cost of the items, have in place a penalty clause. Before entering into an agreement to do the shopping for change, write a note that says:

'If the money supplied does not cover the cost of the required items, then an amount of [insert an amount you think is reasonable] per item will be charged for the inconvenience of an extra trip to the shops, and a further [insert another amount] for the embarrassment caused at the checkout.'

Then get a parent to sign this note and keep it in a safe place. If they ever refuse to pay the extra charge, show them the note with their signature.

Celebrity Note

Groucho Marx, one of the world's greatest comedians, made money by shopping for his mother when he was a kid. Every day, he was sent to the bakery to buy a loaf of bread. He always bought a loaf that had been baked the day before, as it was a nickel cheaper than a freshly baked loaf. He never told his mother that the bread was a day old and he kept the nickel.

I'd like a loaf of that day old bread for 2 nickels instead of 3 please

Sure kid...! But what's with those silly stick-on glasses and moustache?

Nº 25

Jobs around the House

You'll score yourself some extra cash if you dust the table without waking me

Notice how many jobs there are that need to be done around the house? Where there's a job that needs doing, and where there's a tired, worn out-parent, there's a way to make some money.

Tasks That Needs Doing

•vacuuming •washing up •putting out the rubbish •dusting •mopping and sweeping •wiping dirty surfaces •cleaning the bath and shower (and even the toilet) •setting and clearing the table •cooking dinner •making beds •washing and grooming pets •washing windows •outside jobs such as raking leaves, mowing the lawn, washing the car, cleaning gutters, painting fences, gardening, hanging up the washing and taking it down

MAKING MONEY AT HOME

You don't need instructions on how to do these jobs. You've watched your parents do them for years and conveniently ignored them. But now's your chance to get in their good books and earn a bit of money.

Going About Your Work

Ask for a list of jobs that need doing regularly and negotiate a payment for each one. Once you've got a list, make a timetable of chores, so that you don't have to do too much on one day. One small job a day seems easier than six or seven in one day. Make sure you stick to your schedule, otherwise you'll come to the weekend and find that you're going to spend your precious spare time with a mop and broom in your hand, rather than on your bike or with your friends. And remember, do as good a job for your folks as you would for anyone else who's paying you. Just because they're your parents, doesn't mean they can't fire you.

Special Tip...

It's not only your parents who are potential employers. If you have a brother or sister, the chances are that from time to time they're going to have somewhere they want to go but can't until their chores have been done. Let them know that you're always willing to help them—for a cost, of course. And remember, in those situations where they're desperate to go out, you are in the best bargaining position. Negotiate a higher rate of pay.

What's your asking price for doing the PHYSICS Homework as well as the ENGLISH homework while I go to the movies?

'For the past year, I've been earning money just by doing jobs around the house. I do about half an hour every day straight after school and still have plenty of time to see my friends or do my homework (yuk!).'—James

Nº 26

Doing Jobs from Mum's & Dad's Work

Now you're a kid with plenty of spit..! I ran out of time at lunch to stick stamps on these...

Any chance of you... licking and sticking these while I'm out?

If your Mum, Dad or older brother or sister go to work, ask them to keep an eye out for any small jobs that they could bring home for you to do.

Suggestions

Here are a few suggestions of jobs you could do:

• stuffing letters into envelopes • sticking stamps on envelopes
• putting price stickers on goods • wrapping and packing small items

MAKING MONEY AT HOME

You could also offer to go into the office after school and do things like:

•**clean computer screens** •**clean computer mice**
•**clean computer keyboards** •**empty trash bins** •**wash cars in the office car park**

Jobs that can be done in your home usually suit all ages. However, if you have to go into your Mum's or Dad's workplace, there may be a law that says you have to be over a certain age.

Marketing Tip...

Next time you have a large family gathering coming up, prepare some leaflets or business cards. They could read something like:

Give one to every relative at the gathering and when they ask you about it, give them some details about the types of jobs you can do. You never know when you'll get that phone call.

Joey Johnson

General office jobs a speciality
No jobs refused
Reasonable rates
Ring 9999 9999 for more details

'My first ever job was stuffing brochures into envelopes for my Mum's work. She would bring them home and I'd sit in front of the TV doing them. Once Mum's boss knew that I was willing to do odd jobs, I was asked to do more and more jobs, some at home and some at the office. When I wanted a holiday job, I asked my Mum's boss and he hired me on the spot. After all, he already knew that I was a hard worker.'
–Michael

> You've heard of working from home to earn money... well this is working in front of the TV! What more could a kid want!

№ 27 Simple Treatments

You Scratch My Back

The key to giving a good back scratch is to make sure that you scratch hard enough to get rid of the itchiness but not too hard to hurt. While scratching, you should ask the person whether you're scratching too hard or not hard enough. Make sure you scratch over clothing and better still, use a wooden back scratcher.

I'm here about the BACK SCRATCHING job.

How to Give a Head Massage

Here's the best way to give someone a satisfying head massage:

- Get your patient to lie on their back, on a sofa or bed.
- Using the pads of your fingertips, press lightly on each temple and gently rotate.
- Gradually move down to the area behind their ears.
- Move further down until you are rotating your fingers on the back of their neck, then to the base of their spine.
- Next, move up to their forehead. Place your fingertips in the middle of their forehead and slowly move your hands to each side of their face.
- Move down to the area around the eyes. Again, rotate your fingertips slowly.
- Then, massage the area around their cheeks.
- Finally, move up to their head and press your fingers into their scalp. Massage firmly, then rub your hands through their hair.
- Allow them to rest until they are ready to get up.

How to Give a Manicure

Here's the best way to give someone a manicure:

- Remove old nail polish with nail polish remover applied to a cotton ball.
- Dip hands into a solution of warm soapy water, then pat dry with paper towels.
- Rub hands with oil and hand lotion.
- File fingernails into a neat oval shape. Stroke in only one direction.
- Buff the nails.
- Push cuticles back with a cuticle stick.
- Carefully cut away any skin hanging from the side of a fingernail.
- Apply polish.

Marketing Tip...

Offering 'satisfaction guaranteed' when you provide a service is a good marketing idea. It means that if your customer is not happy with the work you have done, they do not have to pay you. However, your customer is more likely to give you a go because they know that you're unlikely to offer such a guarantee if you weren't sure that you could do a good job.

Oh my.../ What have you been doing with these nails? They'll need a little work! But rest assured...my work is guaranteed

Massaging

Massages relieve stress. And everybody hates stress. If you can massage members of your family, you'll benefit in many ways. First, you'll earn money— which is presumably why you're reading this book. Second, you'll be relieving the stress of a parent or brother or sister, which will make you very popular with them (for a short time at least). Third, and most important, you'll be relieving the stress within your household which will make you very popular with everyone else. The less stress in the home, the better.

Types of Massage

There are many different types of massages. Some are purely for relaxation, others to relieve stress, others to relieve sore muscles. To give a proper, professional massage requires a great deal of training and practise. However, the instructions below are for a relaxation and stress relief massage that anyone can give. The best way to find out if you're doing a good job is to ask your patients what they liked best and how you can improve your massages.

How to Give a Foot Massage

Here's the best way to give someone a foot massage:

- Remove their shoes and socks.
- Soak their feet in warm water for about five minutes.
- Rub some oil into your hands and gradually apply to the bottom of their feet.

- Using your thumbs and knuckles, dig hard into the bottom of their feet. Keep doing so until you have covered the entire soles of both feet.
- Place one foot in your lap and dig your thumbs into the top of their feet. Once you have covered the whole area of one foot, repeat with the other foot.
- Rub their feet with a towel and apply baby powder. (If you have a foot spa, you may wish to let them soak the feet for 10–15 minutes before drying and applying powder.)

How to Give a Hand Massage

Here's the best way to give someone a hand massage:

- Rub the back of each hand with the palm of one of your hands.
- Press and rotate the pads of your fingertips over the back of one hand. When the whole area has been covered, separate the fingers and press firmly along the sides of each finger, using your thumb and forefinger.
- Repeat with the other hand.
- Turn the hands over so the palms are facing up.
- Massage the area just below each finger and thumb.
- Grab the end of a finger or thumb and pull firmly but slowly.
- Repeat with each finger and thumb.
- End by massaging right around each wrist.

'I started off giving massages to my sister, Mum and Dad. But as soon as other family members heard about it, they began ringing and making bookings. Now I have cousins popping in almost every afternoon. I think I'll put my price up.'–Alice

Special Tip...

Check with the patient that you are applying the right amount of pressure. Some people prefer a hard massage, others a softer one.

Sure...I can fit you in between 4.35 and 4.40 pm for that massage... O.k... See you downstairs in 5 minutes... bye Mum!

Nº 29

A Weekend Away (at home)

> Would Sir and Madame like Roberto to assist them with their bag? Your bathroom is on the right at the top of the stairs. But then...you know that...it's your house

Most adults love getting away for a weekend but it's never easy with children. So why not suggest they have a weekend away, at home? For the whole weekend, you will treat the house as a hotel and your parents as your guests. And of course, you'll charge them an agreed fee. You'll be happy because you'll be earning money. They'll be happy because they'll be pampered for the weekend for a fraction of the cost of a real hotel.

What to Do

- First of all, get your parents to leave the house so that you can clean their bedroom and the bathroom to the same level as in a hotel. Put a chocolate on each pillow.

- Tidy up the rest of the house, making sure to put a couple of vases of fresh flowers where they'll be noticed.

MAKING MONEY AT HOME

- When your parents arrive back, greet them at the door. Make up a name for the 'hotel' so that you welcome them to 'Hotel Paradise' or whatever name you have come up with.

- Show them around the house and to their room. Ask them if they'd like a drink or other refreshment.

- Present them with a breakfast menu that you have prepared. Allow them to choose what they want for breakfast and the time that they want it served. Offer them the choice of breakfast in bed or breakfast in the dining room.

- Also present them with a list of nearby restaurants. This gives them the opportunity to go out for dinner. Another alternative is a list of take away menus if they wish to eat dinner at home. Of course, if you're confident enough to cook dinner for them, you could present them with a dinner menu. However, they're less likely to relax if they're worrying about you cooking in the kitchen.

- You could also present them with a list of movies that are on nearby.

- If you usually have a babysitter when your parents go out, organise one yourself. That way, if they choose to go out for dinner, they don't have to find a babysitter for you.

- Give them a little bell that they can ring if they need anything.

- Over the weekend, make sure you treat your parents as guests. Don't bother them with questions and requests, like you usually might.

Special Tip...

Make sure an older friend or family member knows what you are doing over the weekend. That way, if you need any help or have a question, you can phone them instead of bothering your parents.

Hi Grandad.. Yes... I know it's only 5.30AM But Mum and Dad are refusing to get out of bed...

I know it's early... But I need to make their bed!

Nº 30

High Grades Mean More Pocket Money

What is it that best motivates you to get high grades? Is it personal satisfaction? Probably not. Is it the desire to get a good start in life? Perhaps. Is it money? Almost certainly. And what is it that your parents want from you more than anything else? High grades. So here's an opportunity for both parties to be happy. It's called a win-win situation.

Yes my boy... That's our deal... The higher your grade the more we pay....

GREAT!! straight A's! Will you take CREDIT CARD for this?

Determining the Price Point

At the beginning of the school year, sit down with your parents and ask them what grade they'd be happy for you to get in each subject. Then, ask them how much they're willing to pay for each grade you get that's higher than the expected grade. If you and your parents can't come to terms over what is an acceptable grade, suggest they use your most recent grades as the starting point. Once you've agreed on the grades and price, it's up to you.

Special Tip...

GREAT! I think I'm IN THE MONEY!

Don't make this suggestion after you've scored straight As. This idea is best for those who know they can improve on their grades.

"I get $50 for each subject I do better in than I did the year before. Last year my parents had to fork out $300."–Mike

Making Money at School

Nº 31

Organising a Colouring Competition

This is a particularly good idea because you get other people to do the work, yet you earn the money.

Sure... for that sort of money you can colour however you like!

How to Make Money

Find an interesting picture that is suitable for colouring in, make a few copies, then advertise a colouring competition with a cash prize. To make money, charge a small fee for entering the competition. Now, this is where you have to be careful. You have to charge an amount that is small enough to encourage lots of entrants but large enough to make sure you are going to more than cover the cost of the prize. You're also going to have to estimate how many people you think will enter the competition.

Of course, this idea is not limited to colouring-in competitions. You can also hold drawing, cartooning and photography competitions.

"The first time I ran a colouring competition, I also acted as the judge. One of the contestants offered me half the winnings if I picked them. Of course I said 'no' but the next time I asked my dad to be the judge.'–Sonya

Special Tip...

It's probably best that you don't judge the competition. If one of your best friends wins the prize, the other entrants may think it was rigged and they won't participate in your next competition. Ask a parent or teacher to be the judge. That way there can be no suggestion of a deal being done.

And the winner of the colouring competition is this lovely........

Dad... you've got my Award winning masterpiece round the wrong way!

Nº 32
Standing in Queue

If you've got friends who value their lunchtime so much they'd rather go without lunch than stand in queue at the canteen, then here's a chance to make a bit of money.

Take all the time you like... I can stay in this queue for a week if I need to... I've got my lunch box, drink bottle and your pile of cash to keep me going.

How it Works

Offer to buy your friends' lunch for them (with their money of course), for a small fee. It's that simple. And seeing as you're going to be standing there for your lunch anyway, it's about the easiest money you'll ever make.

Setting a Fee

You've got to make sure that you don't charge too high a fee, otherwise people won't use you. But then it's also got to be worth your while. In situations like this, quantity is better than quality. In other words, the more customers you have the better. If you buy lunch for ten people, you'll earn ten times the amount than if you buy for just one person. And the amount of work isn't much more.

Special Tip...

If there are certain items that your friends buy every day and which are cheaper at the supermarket, buy them in advance but charge them the same price as the canteen. It's a little extra money in your pocket.

I bought these two strawberry yoghurts from a guy at the canteen who said he got them from a supermarket cheap

What a bargain!

But when did he buy them from the supermarket and how long have they been in his bag?

Nº 33 Compiling and Selling a Magazine

I think I'll start a MAGAZINE ...A School MAGAZINE.... Then buy up a few newspapers... a TV network or 2 ... perhaps retire at 12

Do you fancy yourself as a young Rupert Murdoch? Well, here's a good way to start. The steps involved in compiling and selling a magazine at school are not all that different to those that professional magazine publishers have to take.

Selecting a Subject

First, you have to make sure that the magazine will sell. Even if you're interested in antique furniture, it's unlikely you'll sell many copies if you put out a magazine on that topic. Professional publishers conduct research before putting out a magazine. You can do the same by asking your friends what subjects they would most like to see in a magazine. See, already you're acting like a professional publisher.

MAKING MONEY AT SCHOOL

Finding Contributors

Once you've chosen a subject, you have to find people to research and write articles and provide illustrations or photos. Of course, you can do a lot of this yourself if you have the time and the ability but you may wish to use other people. You're going to have to pay these people, so negotiate a rate that you're both happy with.

Laying Out the Magazine

Once you've got the articles, illustrations and photos, you need to lay them out. In the past, this was a complex process that could be done a number of ways, including taping and pasting the articles together, then taking photos and turning the film into a printed document. Today, there are many computer software packages designed specifically for publishing magazines (and newspapers) and which beginners can easily master. The most common is Microsoft Publisher, which is included in the Microsoft Office suite of products.

Compiling Tips

When putting together your magazine, make sure you put the most interesting articles towards the beginning of the magazine. If people flick through the magazine before buying it, they are more likely to look at what's at the front, rather than what's at the back. Also, put the most striking illustration or photo on the cover, as well as some attention-grabbing headlines. Your aim is to get people interested enough to want to read more.

Setting a Price

Once you've got the magazine published, you have to work out how much to sell it for. You want to set a price that covers your costs and provides a bit extra for your efforts but that is not so high that it turns people off buying it. This is a dilemma that all magazine publishers face.

101 COOL WAYS TO MAKE MONEY   77

Selling the Magazine

Once you've published and printed the magazine, and determined its selling price, you have to sell it. Set up a stand in a prominent place, like the front entrance to school. If there are people who you know are particularly interested in the subject that the magazine covers, seek them out and try to sell it face-to-face. Magazine publishers pay a lot of money to track down people interested in the subjects they write about.

Marketing Tip...

The best method of advertising is word-of-mouth. This involves one person telling someone else how good a product or service is. If someone tells you that they saw a great movie last night and you go along to see it, then the cinema and movie distributor have benefited from word-of-mouth advertising. You could pay some friends a small amount of money to talk about the magazine at playtime and lunchtime. The idea is to create a buzz around the schoolyard that results in people wanting to buy the magazine. This may seem wrong but it's not. It's modern marketing.

> Give me one of those...and I'll tell my friends It's a good magazine. Give me another one...and I'll tell the world it's the best magazine on the face of the Earth

Special Tip...

When you read a magazine, the chances are it's full of advertising. Magazine publishers love advertisers. Advertisers pay money to promote their businesses in magazines. Why not approach local businesses and see if they're willing to take out an advertisement in your magazine? It's extra money for you and it makes the magazine look even more professional.

Making Money on Holiday

No. 34 Bringing Back Those Hard to Find Items

Oh this is RARE! You're not likely to come across another one of these babies! It's the shell of a rare Melanesian land slug... on a string! I've got to ask top money for this one!

GREAT! In that case you wouldn't happen to have a second one would you?

They're pretty rare but I'll see what I can find.

Here's a quick lesson in economics. (Once you've understood this, you'll be able to run the country.) If an item is in great demand but there are few of them, then the seller can ask for a high price. If an item is plentiful, then the price will go down. It's called the law of supply and demand. It's a law that you can take advantage of whenever you go on holiday.

What to Buy

If you're lucky enough to go overseas, locals will offer you many items. If they're things that can't be bought back home, the chances are that you'll be able to sell them for far more than you paid for them. And you can make the law of supply and demand work even more in your favour. Don't buy lots of one item; buy small amounts of many items. If you have five people interested in buying a sea-shell necklace and you only have three of them, you're in a great position to raise the price of the necklaces. However, if you come home with seven sea-shell necklaces and there are only five interested buyers, they're in a position to lower the price. And even if you don't go overseas, look around for the opportunity to buy items that can't be easily found back home.

Customs Warning

Some countries do not allow certain items into their country. Before you plan to bring items from one country into your country, check with your country's department of customs:

1 Which items are restricted.
2 Whether there is a limit on the number of certain items that can be brought in. If you ignore the regulations, you could end up having your items confiscated and having to pay a large fine.

Among the items that may be restricted are:

•**food and plant items** •**protected cultural heritage items** •**toys or other articles containing quantities of lead, mercury or arsenic**
•**wood products**
•**animals** •**weapons**
•**pirated CDs and other illegally copied items**

> You won't find bubblegum like this round here!

> This gum is from OVERSEAS!

> I'll buy what's left of the box!

> 'I'm from Australia and went on a holiday to the United States. While I was there, I bought bubble gum and sweets that I'd never seen at home. On my first day back at school, I turned up with a suitcase full of goodies and had sold them all by the end of the day.'—Ricky

№**35**

★ **Using Metal Detectors**

Well... Some pirate's not going to be too happy that we found this!

BEEP
BEEP
BEEP
BEEP
BEEP
BEEP

Many years ago, the cry was 'there's gold in them thar hills'. Well, today, there may not be quite as much gold in the ground as in the gold rush days but there are other valuables to be found. A great way to pass some time while on holidays, and possibly make a bit of pocket money, is to use a metal detector to find buried treasure.

Choosing a Detector

At some popular holiday destinations, you may be able to hire a metal detector. If not, borrow one from a friend or buy one. Although you may be able to buy a second-hand one cheaply, be aware that the more recent the model, the more effective it will be in detecting hidden treasure. This is because it has been built with more recent technology.

What You Can Find

So what can you find with a metal detector? Well, you may end up with nothing but a few rusty nails and old paperclips. But you may also find coins, jewellery, medals and even rare minerals such as gold. If you buy a metal detector, you probably won't recoup the cost of your purchase on your first holiday but over time it may prove to be a wise investment.

Where are the best places to look for hidden treasure? Well, basically, any place where humans have been present. Beaches, camping grounds, parks and gardens—just about anywhere.

That sounds like an EXPENSIVE beep to me!

BEEP
BEEP
BEEP

How a Detector Works

Metal detectors detect magnetic objects by sending and receiving radio wave signals. When they are directly above such an object they usually emit a beeping sound. Depending on the technology in the detector, they can detect objects up to 20 centimetres (8 inches) below the surface.

'I was at the beach one day, using my metal detector, when a guy asked if I would help look for his car keys. They'd fallen out of his pocket and were hidden in the sand. After just a couple of minutes searching, we found them. He gave me ten dollars for my help.'—Sam

Nº36

Collecting Shells

Well... I'd like to buy this one...
But what would I do with it?
Does it bite?

Collecting shells can be fun. It can also provide some income if you get involved with other collectors who are interested in buying shells from your collection. One way to increase the value of your collection is to collect shells when you are on holiday, far away from where you live. The types of shells you come across are likely to be different from those back home and of great interest to collectors in your area.

Where to Look

Most people look for shells while walking along a large, sandy beach. Although you are likely to find some shells on the beach, you'll have much more success if you look in rock and mud pools near the beach. This is the natural home of many shell varieties. Pay particular attention to bubbles coming up from beneath wet sand. These bubbles indicate a mollusc habitat where shells are likely to be lying.

MAKING MONEY ON HOLIDAY

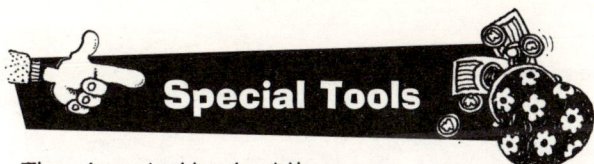

Special Tools

There's no better tool than your eyes and fingers. Look out for shells and pick them up. It can be that simple. However, serious collectors also use:

- **wire screens, to sift sand and therefore collect very small shells** •**a rake, to rake up wet sand in order to uncover shells** •**a note book indicating when the tide comes in and goes out** •**sunscreen, for you, so that you don't get sunburnt**

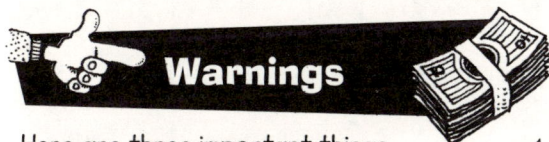

Warnings

Here are three important things to remember when collecting shells.

- All shells were once lived in by creatures. Areas where there are lots of shells are likely to still be habitats for living creatures. Try not to disturb these habitats.

- If you are going to collect shells in a new location, check with the local council or parks and wildlife department if there are areas where shell collecting is not allowed. There may be areas that are under special protection.

- If you are collecting shells from outside your country, make sure that your customs or quarantine department will allow you to bring shells back into your country. If you do not check before you leave, declare your shells when you return, rather than try to sneak them through.

Just lay still and act like a rock and hope that this guy just walks on by and doesn't see us!

I don't want to be part of any shell collection

Making Money from Your Computer Skills

Purchasing, Maintaining and Upgrading Computers

Man! It's just bulging with RAM and the speed of the 30 Gig hard drive is just awesome... 256 mb... 56 kbs modem

I think these guys are from another planet!

56 k modem... that's mean!!

256Mb DDR SDRAM, 30 Gig HDD, 56kbs Modem, 128 Voice 3D Sound.

It may make perfect sense to you but for many people it might as well be Latin. There are so many computers on the market and so many people trying to sell them. To people who don't know much about computers, it can all be very daunting. They can't understand why two computers offering the same features can be such different prices. What they need is someone they can trust who can take matters out of their hands.

Your Skills

To make money by purchasing, maintaining and upgrading computers, you're going to have to be able to:

•**custom build a computer** •**know where to buy reliable second-hand computers** •**know where to buy reliable computer parts** •**know where to buy computer accessories** •**know how to connect all the accessories together**

Understanding Your Customer's Requirements

But most importantly, you're going to have to understand your customer's requirements. This means finding out:

- What they're going to use the computer for.
- Whether they have children who might play computer games that require a lot of memory.
- Whether they want to buy a second-hand or custom built computer or whether they want to pay extra for a model direct from a store.
- Whether they want to pay extra for a guarantee.
- Anything else you can think of that may influence your decisions.
- Of course, once you've bought and installed the computer equipment for a customer, let them know that you're available to fix any problems that may crop up.

How to Charge

There are various ways you can charge for your services. If you're custom building a computer, you can sell it to your customer for more than all the parts cost you. If you find a second-hand computer for someone, you can charge them more than you paid for it. If you're advising someone on which new computer to buy, you can charge them an hourly rate for your time. You can also charge an hourly rate for connecting the computer up or for any maintenance or repairs you carry out.

Warning

Never attempt to rewire any of the power cords or connections. Follow all instructions exactly as they are written. If something doesn't seem to fit, contact the manufacturer or reseller and ask their advice.

Marketing Tip...

After you've supplied and installed a computer for someone, keep in touch with them. Ring them up from time to time and ask how the computer is going. See if they're using the computer more than they expected and for more tasks. If this is the case, they may require an upgrade. And that's where you come in again.

WOOPS

'I've been putting computers together for people for about six years now. It's got to the point where if one of my customers wants to upgrade their computer, I usually know someone who will buy their old one. That means I'm able to earn money from two customers for the one job.'
—Jason

№ 38

Teaching People How to Use Computers and Software

If I push the wrong buttons... Will smoke start streaming from the back of the machine?

Computers are simple to use. Right? Anyone can use a computer. Well, lucky for you, that's not the case. The so-called generation gap means more than just different tastes in music. It means that you can take full advantage of the fact that some people just don't know much about computers but are increasingly being forced to use them.

One-on-One or One-on-More

You can either teach people one-on-one, which means one student at a time, or you can teach more than one student at a time. The advantages of one-on-one teaching are that you can teach in the student's house, which they may prefer; you only have one person to concentrate on; and you can teach at their preferred pace. The advantages of teaching more than one student at a time are that you can earn more money per hour and the students can learn from each other. Of course, there's nothing to stop you teaching both ways: sometimes one-on-one at your house or the student's house; and sometimes more than one student at your place.

If you are going to teach at someone's house, make sure that they are a friend, family member or have been referred to you by someone you know and trust. If you are going to teach someone at your home, make sure a parent or older brother or sister is in the house at all times.

Classes to Offer

There are so many aspects to computing that you can teach. Instead of trying to teach everything at once, why not work out a schedule, print it on a flyer and distribute it. You can include classes on:

•**Computing for Beginners**
•**Understanding MS Word**
•**Understanding Excel**
•**Understanding Email**
•**Surfing the Net**

and any other software or computer technology that you have a good grasp of.

Hmmm....
COMPUTER CLASSES...
I'll keep that flyer
and look into those after
I complete my
Skydiving course

Warning

Computer software companies treat piracy very seriously. Piracy is the illegal use of software. Don't be tempted to install software that you have installed in your system, into another person's system, unless you have the special licence that allows this to occur. You may be offered extra money to do this but the fines for the illegal use of software are far, far more than the money you can earn by doing so.

Marketing Tip...

When you put out a flyer, why not include a few testimonials from past or current students. A testimonial is a comment from a satisfied customer. An example would be: 'I knew nothing about computers before my first class but now, after just three lessons, I'm familiar with most of the common software and have set up an email account. It's all very exciting.'–Maureen Brown, Fairfield

Nº 39

Selling and Installing Software

Load this program onto your computer and you can virtually live your whole life sitting infront of it...

RUN YOUR LIFE for P.C.

As you know, most software is not cheap. That's why people who do not have a great working knowledge of computers are reluctant to either upgrade their old software or try new software. It's not that they don't want to, they just don't want to waste their money on something they might not really need. But if they had a little computer guardian angel who could advise them on what would best suit their needs, then they'd be very happy indeed. Now, where could they find such an angel? You? What a great idea!

MAKING MONEY FROM YOUR COMPUTER SKILLS

Knowing Your Software (and your client)

To be able to choose the right software for someone, you're going to need to be informed about all the latest software: what they do, how much they cost, how reliable they are, whether there are cheaper alternatives, and whether they can be downloaded or have to be bought in pack. You are also going to need to know exactly what your client needs the software for. They may have heard about a particular product from one of their friends and think that they should have it too. However, their friend may have completely different needs to your client. It's your job to direct them towards what they need.

Installing the Software

Of course, once you've helped them to select the right software, they'll probably need someone to install the software for them correctly. And then to show them how to use it. Of course, it costs them a little bit more for every extra service.

Marketing Tip...

It's well known in the marketing world that a loyal, long-term customer is much better than a one-off customer. That's why you should always look after your customers and not get too greedy. If a customer thinks that you're offering a fair price for your services, they're likely to use you over and over again. If you take advantage of someone and charge them too much for software or for your services, they're unlikely to use you again.

The other 49 programs I bought from you and loaded onto my super computer are great... I'm very impressed with your service

I'll take another dozen

Typing/ Word Processing

> I feel like I can't type any faster than snail's pace... Is there anything you can do to speed things up a little?

QWERTYUIOP. If you know what that means, then this is the idea for you. It's the top line of a keyboard and if you recognised it, you're probably pretty good at typing. Lucky for you, there are many, many people out there who wouldn't recognise it and whose typing pace is about as fast as a snail climbing a steep hill.

Latest Software

To set up a typing/word processing business, not only are you going to need to be able to type quickly, you'll probably need to have the latest version of Microsoft Word, the most popular software for word processing.

Things to Type

Once you've spread the word about your business, you may be required to type some of the following:

• **homework and projects** • **resumes** • **reports**
• **letters** • **theses** • **articles**

MAKING MONEY FROM YOUR COMPUTER SKILLS

Knowing the Right Format

You're going to need to know how letters and resumes should be set out and how reports should be formatted. If you're not sure how something should be formatted, check with your customer before you start. You'll just be wasting your own time if you have to re-format a piece of work at the end.

How to Charge

Most typists charge per page or per word. That way the customer knows pretty well from the beginning what it's going to cost them. They don't like paying on an hourly basis because if the typist is slow, they have to pay more.

Special Tip...

When you've finished typing, always use the spell and grammar check tool available on most word processing software. However, if you're at all unsure about the spelling of a word or whether a sentence has been written correctly, make a note of it and check with your customer.

Are you sure it's spelt 'skool'?

Search me!

'Although I was a fast typist, I did a course in Microsoft Word before starting my business. I learnt so much about the program, particularly the formatting options, that I'm completing jobs far quicker than if I hadn't done the course.'—Brianna

Graphic Design

My young daughter can make brochures just like that at home ....but for FREE!

Professional graphic designers have a love-hate relationship with computers. They love the fact that computers make their job easier but they hate the fact that computers also make it easier for other people to produce fancy graphic designs. People like you.

Materials

These days, if you have an artistic eye you can produce all sorts of graphic material, including:

- **invitations** • **thank you notes** • **birth notes** • **promotional flyers**
- **posters** • **business cards** • **logos** • **letterheads**

There are a number of software packages that will guide you through the process, ranging from the simple (such as Publisher) to the more complex (such as Quark).

Understanding What Works

Apart from learning and mastering the relevant software packages, you should have a good understanding of how to use colours, fonts and space on the page to produce the best results. If you're good at art, you're probably well on the way to understanding these. But it still wouldn't hurt to do a short course in graphic design. You'll learn heaps.

You and Your Client

Before starting a job, ask your client the following questions:

- Who is this work aimed at?
- What reaction do you want people to have to this work?
- Can you show me some pieces that you particularly like or are similar to what you want?
- Never complete a job without consulting your client at some stage. It's probably best to show them a couple of ideas early on. That way you can make sure you're on the right track from the outset.

Special Tip...

One great way of learning about graphic design is to look at material around you. This could be marketing material such as junk mail, packaging around products that you buy, advertising posters, corporate logos—anything and everything. Try to work out why you think one design works, while another one doesn't. The chances are, if you think something's particularly good or bad, so will others.

'I was really embarrassed when I went to see a small company about designing their business cards. They asked me for a card of my own and I didn't have one. I went straight home and designed my own business card.'–Sandy

Web Site Design

There might be millions of WEB SITES ... but I'm sure there's room for one more Web Site designer

Move over..! I'm coming ON-LINE!

No-one knows exactly how many web sites there are in the world. There are obviously millions and millions of them, with many more being added every day. Some of them are great, some of them average and some pretty terrible. The best thing for budding web site designers like you is that every business and many individuals think that they have to have a web site. And seeing that most of them have no idea how to go about getting a site up and running, they're going to have to turn to someone. You!

Appearance is Everything

There are two main aspects to designing a web site. The first is the actual physical appearance of the site. Many of the tips that were discussed in 'Graphic Design' are applicable here, particularly the point about having a good understanding of how to use colours, fonts and space on a page to produce the best results. However, there are also a few other things to be aware of. They include making sure that:

• The text is easy to read on screen.

• The site is easy to navigate around.

• There are not so many graphics and special effects that the pages take a long time to download.

Languages and Programs

To be able to design web sites you are also going to have to know several computing languages, particularly HTML, XML and JavaScript. As was suggested in the section on graphic design, it may be a good idea to do a short course.

Most web site designers use particular software programs to help them do their job. Among the software that you could consider using are graphic programs such as Paint Shop Pro and Adobe Photoshop and web editing programs such as Netscape Composer, Microsoft FrontPage and Macromedia Dreamweaver.

Loading a Site

Of course, designing the site is only half the process. You still have to get it loaded onto a server so that it can be viewed by the outside world. If you can do this, as well as design the site, it means you can charge a lot more money than if you can only do one or the other. Web sites are published using a program called File Transfer Protocol or FTP. The program can usually be obtained from the Internet service provider (ISP) who is going to host the site. By following the FTP instructions, you can load the site onto the server a page at a time.

Marketing Tip...

You may think that your job is finished once the site is up and running. But it needn't be. Web sites need updating from time to time. So when you're first talking to a customer, let them know that you are available to update the information on their site whenever they need it done. Ring them every three months and remind them about the need to update, particularly if some of the information on their site becomes out of date.

Do you feel parts of your Website are getting a little... ...shall we say... tired?

Would you like me to...shall we say... ...wake them up a little?

'My approach to customers who aren't sure whether they need a web site is to design and publish a site for free. However, I make the customers sign an agreement that only I can update the information—for a fee of course. Over time, continual updating makes me more money than just doing the initial set up would have.'—Kim

Making Money from Collectibles

Nº 43

Collecting and Selling Coins

I found this coin in the backyard. It's 2,000 years old... but is it still worth anything?

See 'Collecting and Selling Stamps' on page 106 for more information on collecting.

Coin Tips

- Don't clean your coins. Making old coins nice and shiny can destroy their value.
- If you just want to get some dirt off a coin, soak it in soapy water. But don't rub it dry; let it dry in its own time.
- Try and collect a whole set of coins, i.e. all levels of currency within a set. Complete sets sell for a higher price than the individual coins sold separately.
- As with stamps, mistakes increase a coin's value. Common mistakes are a missing or wrong letter or number on the coin face.

Become interested in the types of coins that your customers collect. The beauty of collecting coins, rather than stamps, is that you have the opportunity to collect (and sell) very old coins. Unlike stamps, coins have been around in some countries for thousands of years. Depending where you live, it's also possible to uncover ancient coins in the ground.

Nº 44

Start Collecting Now for the Future

"Thanks Grandad for being a hoarder and not throwing out any of your old junk!"

If your parents and grandparents had kept some of the magazines and toys that they read and played with when they were children, you could now be living a life of luxury—particularly if the items are in the same condition as when they were bought. Now, just because your parents and grandparents weren't thoughtful enough to keep such items when they were younger, there's no reason for you to adopt the same attitude.

What to Collect

• magazines (particularly first editions) • books (particularly first editions) • toys • new and interesting packaging • newspaper clippings and front pages

Increasing the Value

Don't just go straight out and buy everything that you see or you may just end up with a room full of worthless junk. Here are some tips to preserve and increase the value of what you've bought.

MAKING MONEY FROM COLLECTIBLES

- When you buy the first edition of a new magazine, don't read it from cover to cover and pass it to friends. If you are interested in reading it and collecting it, buy two copies. Keep one copy in a plastic bag and don't touch it again. You can read the other one and it won't matter how many tears and creases it ends up with.

- If you hear that a book is being recalled from sale for some reason, try and buy a copy before your local bookshop removes it from the shelves. When books are recalled, it is usually for legal reasons. Another edition will be released with the offending material taken out. Any copies of the original version will be worth considerably more than they cost.

- If there's a particular toy that you think may be worth something in the future, don't even take it out of its box. Today, the price of an old Barbie doll or Matchbox car is far higher if it is still in its original packaging.

- Every now and again, manufacturers like to try and change the look and packaging of their products. Sometimes these changes work, other times they don't. If a popular product changes its packaging, buy it but don't open it. If the new packaging does not result in extra sales, the packaging will be changed again and your purchase could be worth a fair bit in the future.

- Sometimes newspaper editors get their front page stories very wrong. In 1948, the Chicago *Daily Tribune* had a headline reading, 'DEWEY DEFEATS TRUMAN', following the presidential election between Harry Truman and Thomas Dewey. Although Dewey was ahead in the voting when the newspaper was published, results that came in later in the night saw Truman become president. Copies of the *Daily Tribune* with that headline are very valuable. In Australia, a similar thing happened on the night of the 1993 federal election when the Melbourne *Sunday Herald Sun* went to press declaring John Hewson the winner. Unfortunately for them, the early voting patterns had changed by the time the night was through. Therefore, on the morning after a close election, rush to your newsagent/newstand and see if any of the early editions got it wrong.

What are you looking for?

NEWS
ELECTION WIN

MISTAKES... It will make this paper worth a lot of cash!

- Of course, collecting for the future is only for those who are patient and have strong will power. It's not for those who enjoy a midnight snack and are likely to eat a 15-year-old chocolate bar hidden on the top shelf of the cupboard.

Collecting and Selling Cards

I'll give you all of my pocket money for a year... plus everything in my lunchbox for THAT card!

I've just got to have it !

Does that include those peanut butter sandwiches and the squashed banana?

Collecting and trading cards has been a popular pastime for a long time. As any card collector knows, the really valuable cards are those that are in short supply. Possessing a card that few people have makes you a very popular person. Collectors will throw money at you. Sounds good, doesn't it? But how do you get such cards?

Know Your Product

A band called the Saints had a song called 'Know Your Product'. In essence, that's the key to collecting. There are so many types of cards on the market that almost every subject is covered. They include:

•football •baseball •basketball •cricket •movies •television •comics and cartoons •music •cars •motorbikes •aircraft •military equipment

and so on and so on and so on.

There's no way that anyone could gain a thorough understanding of every card series. It would means hours and hours and hours of study. It's far better to concentrate on one series or a few similar series. That way you'll be able to learn the true value of the cards and be in a position to make money.

Turning Cards into Money

The way to make money from cards is to buy a card from one person and sell it to another at a higher price. It's that easy. Cards can be bought from friends, special fairs, collectible shops or at collectible auctions. Of course, you don't have to buy cards all the time. You can swap cards. But don't just swap one card for another. More valuable cards should be swapped for two or more less valuable cards. Again, it's important that you understand the true value of your cards. Although swapping is fun, if you want to make money from cards, at some stage you are going to have to move from swapping to selling.

Special Tip...

If you want to make money, don't get too attached to your cards. Some collectors have favourite cards that they don't want to part with. That approach just doesn't make good business sense.

No... I can't part with this card... it's worth big money ... it's rare! You won't see another one!

You can have my lunch!

It's yours!

'I went to a collectible fair looking for a particular card. I needed this card to complete a set. One dealer had the card on display at a price of $50. It seemed so much but I asked the dealer how much I could get for the complete set. He said it was probably worth about $300. So I bought the card for $50 and a week later sold the whole set to another collector for $320. That was the best $50 I ever spent.' –Tony

Collecting and Selling Stamps

In 1996, a Swedish stamp was sold to a collector for over two million US dollars. Now obviously this was no ordinary stamp but it goes to show that there is money in stamps. Most people collect stamps simply as a hobby. They usually collect stamps from particular countries or on a particular topic and they enjoy chasing after stamps they have heard about but which they have never seen. Although they may one day sell their stamp collection or part of it, they are not really in it for the money.

Collecting Rules

Some people, though, collect stamps purely to sell. These people have several rules that are worth considering if you want to make money by selling stamps. These rules include:

• Sellers need buyers. Get to know other stamp collectors because they are your future customers.

MAKING MONEY FROM COLLECTIBLES

- Stamp clubs are a great place to meet potential customers.

- Once you know who your customers are, find out what stamps they collect. There's no point trying to sell British stamps to someone who specialises in Australian stamps. Collect what your customers collect.

- Special edition stamps and first day covers are popular among collectors. Let your local post office know that you're a collector, so they can inform you of special releases.

- Keep your stamps in as good a condition as possible. Be particularly careful when removing stamps from envelopes. Some collectors keep the entire envelope, rather than risk damaging the stamp.

- If something is wrong with a stamp, don't throw it away. It's probably worth more than a normal stamp. When mistakes are made in the printing process, such as stamps printed upside down or the colours running together, the post office usually destroys them. This means that those that slip through the net are very rare and valuable. The Swedish stamp that sold for over two million dollars was a yellow stamp that should have been green.

AHHRR! That stamp is no good...! It's the wrong colour! How did that get in there?

An UNTRAINED STAMP COLLECTOR making her first big mistake

- If you have some very rare stamps, take photos of them to show to people. That way you're less likely to lose them.

- Finally, read as much as you can about stamps and stamp collecting. The more you learn, the more likely you'll recognise when a stamp is selling for less than its true worth.

'I have a note book in which I write how much I paid for each stamp in my collection. That way I know how much I need to sell it for to make a profit. Without such a book, it's hard to keep track.'—Lucy

Nº **47**

Collecting and Selling Autographs

Here! I've signed this piece of paper for you... I might be famous one day and it might be worth some cash!

Unlike coins and stamps, autographs don't necessarily become more valuable the older they get.

Who to Chase

The most sought-after autographs are usually those of the current popular entertainers and sports stars. Because some musicians, actors, television personalities and sports stars have only a short time at the top of their field, it is important to sell their autographs while they are at their peak. A couple of years down the track and it's possible that no-one will be interested in them—except perhaps their mothers. However, there are some exceptions. They include:

- people involved in important historical events
- people who died at their peak

- people who died in a strange or controversial manner
- people who become cultural icons, e.g. Marilyn Monroe
- people involved in scandals

Autograph Tips

Here are some tips for people wanting to make money by collecting and selling autographs.

- Keep an eye on who the most popular personalities are. If you're not up to date with your information, you're not up to date with what your customers want.
- Attend publicity signings, promotional appearances etc.
- Join fan clubs of popular personalities.
- Signatures on photographs and documents are worth more than a signature on a blank piece of paper.
- When buying autographs, beware of fakes.

Special Tip...

Some web sites, such as www.stararchive.com, provide addresses for thousands of celebrities. Writing to these celebrities requesting a photo and/or autograph often works.

I was going to ask you for your autograph.... But I guess my pen's out of ink!

'I take a pen and spare paper with me wherever I go. You never know when you might see a celebrity. Also, if I see a musician or television personality who is just starting out, I always get their autograph. Some of them end up becoming famous.'—Tina.

№ 48 Cleaning Computers

Man!! Is this a computer keyboard... or a lunchbox?

Prepare to be grossed out. You wouldn't believe how dirty people's computers get. People spend so much time in front of computers, eating and drinking as they work, that all sorts of junk find their way between the keyboard keys, inside the mouse and onto the monitor screen.

What Needs Cleaning

There are three main pieces of computer equipment that need cleaning: the keyboard, the monitor screen and the mouse. You should also wipe a slightly damp rag around the outside of the hard drive but leave the insides of the computer alone. You won't be very popular if you cause data to be lost.

Equipment

You're going to need:

- window/glass cleaning spray • paper towels • a cloth
- rubbing alcohol • cotton buds • a pair of tweezers
- a bowl of warm water • a can of compressed air

Cleaning the Keyboard

- Turn the keyboard upside down and shake dust and loose grime out of it.
- Spray compressed air in between keys.
- Dab a cotton bud in rubbing alcohol and wipe in between keys.
- Wipe the surface of the keys with a towel soaked in rubbing alcohol.

Cleaning the Monitor Screen

- Spray some window/glass cleaning spray on a towel and wipe the screen clean.
- Use a clean, dry cloth to wipe any spray residue left on the screen.
- Laptop computer screens are more sensitive than desktop computers. On laptop screens, just use a cloth dipped in warm water.

Cleaning the Mouse

- Remove the mouse ball and rinse in a bowl of warm water.
- Use a pair of tweezers to remove the build-up from the rollers.
- Use a cotton bud dipped in rubbing alcohol for a final wipe of the rollers.
- Dry the mouse ball and put back in place.
- Finally, wipe the outside of the mouse clean with a cloth rinsed in warm water.

Cleaning Mouse Pads

Mouse pads pick up plenty of dirt. The best way to clean a mouse pad is to pick it up and whack it free of grime and dust. Then wipe clean with a dry cloth. However, mouse pads are relatively cheap and should be replaced regularly. That's because the dirt that accumulates on the pad will eventually make its way into the mouse.

How about getting some mouse pads manufactured with your business details on them? Then, when you come across mouse pads that need to be replaced, you can leave one of your mouse pads behind. It's a cheap form of marketing.

General Tips

- Always turn off computer equipment before starting to clean.
- Check the manufacturer's instructions for each item before cleaning them. If their instructions differ markedly to those above, follow their instructions.

Marketing

Prepare flyers and letter-box them to businesses in your area. Make a note of the businesses that you send a flyer to and either ring them up or visit them in person about a week after they've received their flyer.

Marketing Tip...

Offer businesses a free trial. Once you've cleaned their computers once, they'll probably be so impressed with the difference that they'll ask you to come back in about a month to do it again—this time for money.

You've made such a great job of cleaning the office computers... ...they're so sparkly and bright..! I'll need to keep these dark glasses on around the office

By the way... How do they look on me?

№ 49 Installing Fish Tanks in Offices

Would you have something a little more friendly looking? I don't like the way that one's looking at me!

This is a good idea to try at most work places, though you'd probably be wasting your time trying it out at an aquarium or fish shop.

What to Do

Colourful fish swimming around in a tank can be an attractive addition to an office or shop. Your job is to set up a tank with the right type of fish and convince an office or shop to buy it from you, so that you make a profit on your costs and time.

Visit a pet store and speak to someone about the best tank and fish for your needs. Some fish are better suited to particular weather conditions. Also, some fish do not get on with each other. Once you've set up a tank and sold it to a business, remember to give them instructions on caring for the fish. Or you could offer to care for the fish and clean the equipment—for more money, of course.

Fishy Tips

Here are a few tips on keeping fish:

- Don't put too many fish in a tank.
- Put plants, rocks and other adornments in the tank to give the fish places to hide and play.
- Wash gravel before you place it into a tank, or else the grime and dirt will end up in the water.
- Do not overfeed the fish. Any food remaining a couple of minutes after feeding should be removed.
- Change water regularly.
- Do not add too many new fish into the tank at the same time. Certainly no more than four.

Marketing Tip...

Most businesses will take convincing that they need a fish tank. So why not offer them a week's free trial? Put a tank with fish in the office or shop and by the end of the week, they may decide to keep it. Remember to tell your friends and family to visit the shop and office during that week and comment on how good the fish tank looks.

Expenses and Profits

You need to buy a tank, a pump and other cleaning equipment. And don't forget the fish. The amount that you eventually charge will depend on how much money and how much time you've spent on getting everything together. Remember that you can make more money by offering to feed the fish and clean the equipment.

Hmmm... I could swear I had one more sandwich left for lunch. There's some strange things going on around this office!

№50

Producing Marketing Material

Marketing a business is easy. Just get Tiger Woods to put in an appearance. But if the business hasn't got a spare million dollars, or if Tiger is busy playing golf on the day he's required, then there has to be another approach. Most small businesses would love to market themselves more but do not have a person spare who can spend the time required to do it properly. What they need is a helping hand. You!

Well I can't get a Golf Pro here for you... but I could write you some material that would attract as much attention.'

Marketing Tasks

Once you've got yourself a client, the first thing to do is sit down with them and ask them how much they want you to do. The tasks involved in producing marketing material are:

•writing •designing •printing •distributing

Your client may only want you to take care of one of these aspects, though they may want you to take care of two or more. The more you can take care of, the easier it is for your client and the more money you can earn. It's unlikely that you can do all of these tasks brilliantly, so employ friends who are good at those things that you're not so hot at. Many marketing people act as project managers and don't do any of the writing, design, printing or distributing. They organise others to do it.

Who, What and When

There are four key pieces of information that you need to get from your client before you begin producing any material. They are:

- Who their target audience is.
- What messages they want to get across.
- What sort of design they have in mind.
- When they want the marketing material to go out.

Getting Down to Work

Marketing Tip...

If you want to get into the marketing business, you have to start with yourself. If you can't market yourself (and your own business), then others are unlikely to give you a go. Produce your own quality marketing material that shows you can do the job.

Once you've got that information, you're ready to start.

- Writing involves getting the words right. They have to get the message across simply and without confusion. This may take several drafts, in consultation with the client.

Maybe the brochure I designed worked too well.... I can't even get in to return my own video!

- Designing involves getting the look right. The design must be striking and match the message but must not take too much attention from the words.

- Printing involves finding a professional printer who will produce quality material at the cheapest price. Always get quotes from at least two different printers and ask to see other work that they have produced.

- Distribution involves getting the marketing material to the target market. This may involve letter boxing the material, handing it out in shopping centres, mailing it out or just having it lying around in the client's business.

> 'I produced a brochure for the local video store. In the month after it went out, their business increased by 10%. They told some of the other shops, who rang me up to do brochures for them.'–Esther

No 51 Researching the Competition

Market research is very big business. It helps companies understand what their customers want. It can also help them understand what their competitors are offering. Gathering information on a competitor is not illegal. It's good business.

What to Find Out

Once a client agrees to take you on, it's your job to find out what their competitors are up to. This could involve:

- Checking the prices of the competitors' goods and services.
- Finding out about special deals they have on offer.
- Collecting competitors' marketing material.
- Watching out for competitors' advertisements.
- Finding out if competitors have any sponsorship deals.

Using the Information

All of this information can help your client in various ways, such as:

- Matching or beating the competitors' prices.
- Producing better, more eye-catching marketing material.
- Offering special deals better than their competitors are offering.
- Raising their profile by signing sponsorship deals with local sports clubs or other organisations.

Marketing Tip...

Most businesses wouldn't even think about hiring a market researcher to check up on their competitors. Why not walk into a business and ask them if they know that a competitor is offering their goods and services for a particular price? It might take several visits from you but eventually the owner or manager may realise that they can use your information to increase their business.

Special Warning

Although it might be tempting to share your information with two or more companies in the same business, it's not the done thing. A market research business depends on trust and confidentiality. Without these, you won't have a business.

Sport and Entertainment

Nº52

★ ★ Street ★ ★ Performances

Some of the tips in the section on busking are appropriate here. However, street performances include far more than playing instruments. If you have a talent for any of the following, you can perform on the streets:
• dancing • juggling • comedy
• acrobatics • mime • clowning

> Say buddy! You haven't got the time have you?

A Few Tips

Although each of these areas has its own performance techniques, there are a few general tips.

• Create a relationship with the audience. There's nothing worse than a street performer who ignores their audience.

• Involve the audience but don't embarrass them. Embarrassed people are less likely to give you money.

• Don't let your routine go on for too long. People are more likely to give money at the end of a routine but they may not have time to hang around for 20 minutes.

Special Tip...

Watch other street performers. It's the best way to learn. If you see a street performer who has an audience eating out of his or her hands, try to work out what it is that has made the audience react in such a way. Then do it yourself, but add some individual touches.

> You must think my act is pretty good...! You've been standing there watching me all day! Do you like the piano accordian?

> No... I can't stand it... I'm taking notes to start my own show!

No 53

★ Busking ★

If you're the type of person who mimes to your CDs in the privacy of your bedroom, then perhaps it's time for you to share your talents with the rest of the world. Busking is fun, a great way to gain confidence, a fantastic way to make money and there is even the possibility that a world famous record producer will walk past and sign you up to a five CD deal worth millions. Well, perhaps the last part is a bit unlikely but the rest of it is true.

I've got the microphone ... the hat to put the money in ... I've got the rhythm....! Now all I need is to learn to sing.... So as to not scare away the audience!

What it Involves

Busking involves playing instruments or singing on the street. Well, not exactly on the street because then you might get run over, but certainly on the side of the road or in a shopping mall. Some buskers perform on their own, others as a duo, trio or group. Some sing, others play instruments. Some use backing tapes or CDs, others are unaccompanied. The message is simple: if you can sing or play an instrument well, give it a go.

Starting Out

Before you play a single note, remember to:

• Choose a good location. Where there's a crowd there's an opportunity. There's no point setting up outside your house if you live on a farm and no-one ever passes by. So, choose a busy location.

- Get a permit. Some councils only allow buskers to operate if they have a special licence. Ring your council and find out if you need one.
- Find out if there are any noise restrictions. This tip is essential for heavy metal and punk bands.
- Take a hat or box for people to put money in.

A Few More Tips

- Arrive early. If you've picked a popular spot, it's likely other buskers will be interested in it.
- Thank people who give you money. This may be difficult if you play a trumpet and you're in the middle of a Louis Armstrong impersonation but at least make a gesture. The same person may pass by on another day and they'll remember if you didn't acknowledge them.
- Enjoy yourself. Buskers who look as if they're performing for fun and not for money usually end up with more money.

CLUNK CLUNK

Excuse me sonny! Do you take credit card? I love that tune but I'm out of change...!

Thankyou

'I busked to make enough money to buy a couple of Christmas presents. From two Saturday mornings at my local shops, I made enough to buy presents for my whole family. I couldn't believe it.'—Tracey.

Nº 54

Entering Competitions

I wrote a slogan for our school Fair and won 1st PRIZE! I think I'll be selling the prize for cash.

The saying, 'You've got to be in it to win it', certainly applies to entering competitions. While some people think there is no chance they'll win a competition, others spend hours every week trying to prove them wrong. Entering competitions doesn't always result in making money directly, but it can earn you prizes that can then be sold.

A Few Tips

There are so many types of competitions you can enter. The most successful competition entrants specialise in competitions that best suit their skills. Some people are good at word puzzles, others at mathematical puzzles, some at writing slogans, others at answering general knowledge questions. Here are a few to tips to increase your chances of winning good prizes.

- Only enter games of chance when there is no entry fee. Games of chance are those where a name or ticket is chosen at random.

- Work out what type of competitions you are most likely to win.
- If you enter word competitions such as crosswords and word puzzles, you'll need a standard dictionary, a thesaurus and specialist crossword dictionaries.
- If you enter competitions that require the answering of general knowledge questions, you'll need an encyclopedia, an atlas and other reference books. You could use a good web site search engine, such as www.google.com.
- Follow competition instructions exactly. If the rules of a competition state that your entry should be enclosed in a standard sized envelope, don't send it in a larger envelope. You won't get past stage one.
- Enter competitions that have a number of prizes, instead of just one prize.
- Write your answers and name and address very clearly. Judges won't waste too much time if they can't read your handwriting.

Special Tip...

The popularity of the Internet has meant that many competitions require entries to be submitted by email or for competitors to provide an email address. Many of these competitions are held primarily so that companies can obtain email addresses for marketing purposes. They will then send information about their goods and services. If you do enter a lot of competitions that require an email address, consider setting up an email address just for this purpose. That way your regular email inbox (or that of your parents) will not be full of promotional material.

'I've won prizes in about a dozen competitions. I've kept a couple of the prizes for myself, given away three or four as birthday presents and managed to sell the rest to friends at school.'—Michael

Nº 55

Appearing in Television Commercials

If you think you're up to eating 50 cans of baked beans, one after the other, or laughing on cue for three or four hours, then perhaps you should consider doing television commercials. If you think it's glamorous and an easy way to make some money, it's not. However, it does pay well for those with the right qualities and attitude.

> I don't think I can swallow another bean. There goes my plans of becoming a baked bean commercial super star!

Those Special Qualities

The good thing about television commercials is that you don't have to be drop-dead gorgeous to appear. If you watch a lot of television, you'll notice commercials featuring people of all shapes, sizes and colour. Commercials are far more representative of society than actual programs. But those who appear in commercials do share certain qualities. These include:

- patience (it takes a very long time to film a commercial)
- obedience (you have to do exactly what you're told)
- good humour (it can become pretty tense when things aren't going exactly to plan)
- flexibility (a director may change the script or instructions at any moment)
- level-headedness (you're not a Hollywood superstar, at least not yet)

Finding Work

To get work in a television commercial, you're going to have to get yourself an agent. An agent is a person who represents actors and tries to find them work. You'll find a list of agents in the Yellow Pages, probably under the category 'Casting Agencies'. Before sending them any material, ring them up and find out what they require. In general, you'll need to send a professional photo, a list of any acting work that you've done and a letter explaining why you want to do commercials.

Marketing Tip...

Many people use television commercials as a way to begin an acting career. As a result, they've had little or no acting experience. If you've got no experience, take a few acting lessons and put the details in your letter to agents. They're more likely to take notice of someone who has had lessons, than someone who has never done anything.

Being a Movie Extra

Hey Mum! That's me back here! One of the extras!

I'm in a MOVIE mum!

Your son's a STAR!

'Lights. Camera. Action.' If these three words thrill you, consider getting work as a film extra. Film extras are those people who appear in the background of scenes. Sometimes there are hundreds of them making up a large crowd, other times there may just be a few people sitting in the background of a restaurant scene. But be warned: being a film extra can be extremely boring. It can take a whole day to film one scene. That means the extras have to stand in the background or repeat certain actions over and over and over again, often wearing heavy costumes and make-up under hot lights.

Finding Work

As with television commercials you need to send a photo, a list of acting jobs and a cover letter to a few agents. If you're lucky, some of the agents will get you in and have a chat. They may even ask you to act out a particular scene for them. If you're talented, persistent and luck is on your side, an agent may sign you up. That doesn't mean they have work for you straight away, they just want to put you on their books.

A film is cast by a casting agent. The casting agent contacts agents and tells them the number and type of people they want in their film. The agents then go through their books looking for the correct types and send photos and details of their choices to the casting agent. It is no use contacting a casting agent directly. They almost always only accept actors through agencies.

Marketing Tip...

If you're trying to get an agent and are appearing in an amateur theatre production, invite a few agents along to see you. Send them an official invitation, then ring them a couple of times. Some agencies have people whose main job is to see the talent in action. And if they do agree to see you, make sure you put their name on the free list.

We'd like you to sign on the line for a 5 year Movie deal!

We'll offer you a 5 year movie deal too! Plus your own personal limosine for you and your friends with popcorn and drinks

'The best part about being an extra (other than the money) is meeting the stars. I always thought the stars would be too busy and stuck-up to talk to extras but most of them take the time to say hello.' —Nicky

Nº 57 Putting on Film Shows

This is a great idea for people who live in communities where there is no movie theatre. Even if you live in a big city, it can be fun to arrange a film night. Many people only watch movies on television or video, while others find big cinema complexes to be impersonal.

I'll be right along with your POPCORN and DRINKS. I just need to find somewhere to plug in the projector!

The Show Must Go On

Putting on a film show involves a lot of organisation. These are the jobs that have to be done:
•**booking a venue** •**hiring a film** •**hiring the equipment** •**advertising the night** •**selling tickets** •**selling refreshments** •**running the film** •**cleaning the venue**

Equipment and Expertise

To run the film you're going to need:
•**a projector** •**a screen**
•**speakers** •**someone with the knowledge to connect all the equipment up and make sure it works properly**

'A friend and I put on a film in the local scout hall one Friday night. It proved such a success that we did it again the following Friday night. Then the next. Then the next. We've been operating for three years now and the Friday night movie has become a major event in our town.'—Amy

Special Tip...

When you're choosing a film, think hard about the audience you're trying to attract. If you want families to attend, you need a film that will not be too violent for young children but will not be too childish for adults. Some communities screen movies that were made in or near their town.

Hey...! That looks just like you in this movie!

I know... I filmed, financed, produced, edited and starred in this film... and yes... that is our backyard!

I hate scary movie

№ 58

Lending a Hand at Local Sports Events

I hope the kid with the great kick continues to boot the balls way down the back of the field....

He's helping me earn loads of cash!

It's not only professional sporting teams that require extra people to make sure the game goes smoothly. Amateur teams require just as many people. The only difference is that amateur teams rely on volunteers—usually family and friends of the players.

How to Get Work

If you live near a sports ground where local matches are played on weekends, take a walk down in the morning and ask if anyone needs help setting up equipment. Then, during the day, approach team officials and ask if they need a helping hand. You could run water onto the ground, fetch balls, mark out lines, help officiate or take on any other job that you or they can think of. Make sure that you make it clear that you expect to be paid and determine the price (and the person who will pay you) before you start.

Marketing Tip...

Set up a small stall at your local sports ground and put up a sign reading 'Helping Hand for Hire'. That way, anytime anyone needs help throughout the day, they'll know who to use and where to find them.

Nº 59 Setting up a Stall at a Festival or Local Event

Sorry...you'll have to wait a while. The popcorn is still a little volatile!

HOT POPCORN

Isn't it great when a festival or other event is held near your home? You get to hang out with your friends, check out the stalls, buy some goodies, perhaps listen to some music and generally have a lot of fun. Well, think how much more fun it would be if you could make some money out of it. Here's how to go about getting involved.

Getting Involved

- Keep an eye out for advertisements or notices about local festivals and events.
- Contact the organisers and ask if you would be able to set up a stall. The organisers may ask for a fee, so before you ring, work out whether or not you're willing to pay.

- If you do get permission, find out as much as you can about the event, then organise your stall to fit in with the general theme. For example, if it's a festival to celebrate the start of a particular season, set up a stall with food that is associated with that season.

- On the day, set your stall up nice and early. You'll need some tables, chairs for you to sit on (it could be a long day), a money box or small tin safe, some change, a sign advertising what you're selling and, of course, your goods.

- You also might need some special equipment, depending on what goods you're selling. If you're selling food that should be served cold, then you'll need some eskies or a small fridge connected to a power source.

- Smile and be polite. The customer is always right.

Marketing Tip...

Think outside the square. That means don't just go with the obvious choice. Try to think of a product or service to sell that others won't be offering.

'Our council put on an olive festival last year, in some parkland that contained some olive trees. There was plenty of music and entertainment and lots of stalls. Four of us set up a stall selling pasta, with olive oil, garlic and cheese. It was a huge success.' –Jenn

№60 Selling Car Park Spaces

Hey...! You in the red car! Mind my Dad's paintwork!

PARKING AVAILABLE BETWEEN MY DAD'S AND MUM'S CARS

CASH

There are advantages and disadvantages in living near a sporting or entertainment venue. One advantage is that it's not too far for you to go if you're interested in the event that's on. One disadvantage is that hundreds or even thousands of people may trample the lawn outside your house every week. If your lawn is getting ruined anyway, why not try and make some money out of it?

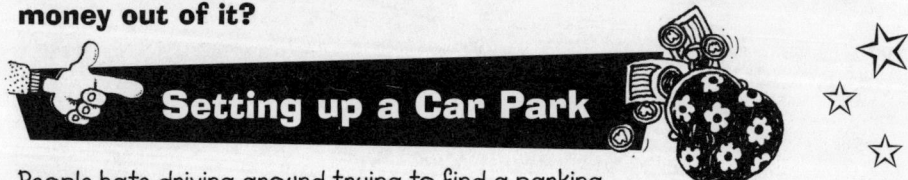

Setting up a Car Park

People hate driving around trying to find a parking space, so put up a sign welcoming cars to park on your lawn and even in your driveway, for a fee of course. (Ask your parents first. They may not be too impressed to look out the front window and see a parking lot outside.)

SPORT AND ENTERTAINMENT

Other tips:

- Before you decide how much to charge, visit the nearest car parks and see how much they charge. Make sure your fee is considerably lower.

- Fit as many cars as you can onto your lawn and in your driveway. However, there has to be enough room for each one to get out, without having to shift other cars around.

- Leave a piece of paper with your phone number on the windscreen. That way, when the car owners are coming to another event, they can ring ahead and book. Every business knows that regular customers are the best customers.

- Offer extra services such as washing and vacuuming the car.

Special Tip...

At the bottom of your sign, write in small letters: 'All care is taken but no responsibility is taken for any damage'. That way you are covered if one driver hits another car.

What does that say at the bottom of that sign...?
NO SKIDDING UP DAD'S GRASS...
NO SQUASHING MUM'S FLOWERS
and NO PARKING ON ANY OF
THE 7 GARDEN GNOMES!

PARKING HERE!
ON OUR LAWN

Yep.. Fair enough... sounds O.K to me!

Marketing Tip...

Try and be outside when the event finishes, so that you can thank your customers. Apart from being good service, you may get a tip from them— particularly if they're in a good mood because their team has just won.

101 COOL WAYS TO MAKE MONEY   135

Nº 61 Selling Refreshments/ Programs at Events

'Popcorn!' 'Programs!' 'Hot dogs!' 'Cold drinks!' Yell these out a few times and you're well on your way to earning pocket money as a program or refreshments seller at major events. Today, almost every event, whether it be a theatre show, a sporting event or a concert, has people selling programs and refreshments. Few of these jobs are full-time jobs, making them ideal for students. Because many of them take place at night and on weekends, you need to be available at these times. However, some companies will allow you to choose the shifts that you want.

Being Effective

To be able to be an effective seller at events, you need to be able to do the following:

•**serve people quickly and politely** •**quickly work out how much change people should get** •**have a strong voice to shout out what you're selling** •**ignore rude customers**

Payment

With most of this type of work, your ability to sell will determine your income. You will probably get paid a percentage of your sales. This is called a commission. However, you may be guaranteed a minimum payment, which is called a base payment.

'I sell food and drinks at a concert venue. While all my friends save up their money to see bands, I get paid to be there. Although I'm working, it's always great fun.'–Marcus

Getting a Job

Although some venues hire their sellers directly, most of them contract the work out to other companies. The best way to find out whom you should approach is to ring the venue you are interested in working at and ask which company hires part-time sellers. Once you've got those details, ring the relevant company and ask how to apply. Some may want you to send a letter first, others may ask you in for an interview.

Interview Tip...

There are four major things to remember when preparing for an interview.

• Dress smartly.
• Speak clearly.
• Be polite.
• Always have a question ready to ask at the end of the interview.

Ok...! Let me hear you say – HOT DOGS REALLY LOUD!!

Do you want me to say that with sauce?

Collecting and Selling Golf Balls

Boy! This is more profitable than just raking boring old leaves

If you live near a golf course, you've probably found stray balls in your street or even in your garden. But have you considered making some money from golfers who can't hit straight?

Collecting the Balls

There are two ways to collect golf balls: on the course and off the course. By collecting stray balls in the streets around the course, you do not have to ask anyone's permission. However, you may walk around the entire outside of the course without finding any stray balls. An easier way is to collect lost balls on the golf course. To do this, you are going to have to ask the permission of the golf course owner or manager. It may be that other kids are already doing it and your name will be put on a waiting list.

When collecting golf balls on the course, stick to the trees, bushes and water hazards. You should carry a rake (for looking in long grass) and a pole with a net on the end (for looking in water hazards). When you spot a stray ball, don't pick it up immediately, but make sure there is not a golfer walking towards the spot, looking for their ball.

Adding Value

To get the best price for old golf balls, clean them up before selling them. Warm soapy water and a washing up brush should do the trick. But be careful not to scrub off any of the enamel. Chipped golf balls can't be sold for much.

Selling the Balls

The best person to sell your golf balls to is the owner or manager of the golf course. They can then sell them on to golfers. You won't get as much money for each ball as you would selling them directly to golfers but you'll get rid of them quickly, leaving you plenty of time to find more. If the golf course owner or manager does not want to buy them from you, set up a stall near the golf course with a large sign saying 'Golf Balls for Sale. Good Quality, Cheap Prices'. This should attract a few golfers on their way to the course.

Gee that looks just like Betsy my favourite old golf ball I shot over the trees in last week's game...

Boy... I really miss wacking that old girl around the course

REALLY CHEAP GOLF BALLS

Caddying

I hate to sound like a... I told you so... But I did tell you to use a 5 IRON!

'Hey Tiger, I think you should use a five iron, not that seven iron.'

'Sure, caddy. I'll do as you say.'

Quit dreaming. This could be you.

What Caddies Do

Caddying is a job for kids who love golf or who wish to know more about the game. If you're not interested in golf, you won't last long. The only thing people on the course want to talk about is golf. And they take it seriously.

If you think caddies just carry a golfer's clubs around, think again. Caddying also involves:

•**keeping the clubs and balls clean** •**advising on which clubs to use** •**working out the distance from the hole** •**raking the sand in bunkers** •**watching where the ball goes after being hit** •**determining the strength and direction of the wind**

How to Get Started

Ring up a few golf courses in your area and ask about caddying. Some golf clubs have training sessions for new caddies. Others may tell you just to turn up at a certain time and wait for a player who wants a caddy. Once you've caddied for someone a couple of times, they may want you regularly. If this occurs, they'll inform you when and where they're playing next.

Behaviour

Golfers and golf clubs expect certain behaviour, knowledge and attitudes from caddies. These include:

•**punctuality** •**politeness** •**conforming to the club's dress code** •**understanding the game** •**knowing the characteristics of the particular course**

Special Tip...

Before setting out for a day's caddying, check the weather report. If it's going to be sunny, take a hat and sunscreen. If it's going to be cold and rainy, dress appropriately. A game of golf takes about four hours. That's a lot of time to be facing the elements.

And don't forget to take some food and drink. Be sure to dispose of any rubbish thoughtfully. Better still, take it away with you.

Hmmm.... Is there something my caddy knows about the weather that I don't?

'I started caddying when I was 13. I loved golf and thought it would be a great way to make a bit of money. Ten years later, I work as a professional caddy, travelling around the globe and watching the world's best golfers close-up. Do I like it? No, I love it.'—Sam

Anyone for Tennis? Ball Boys and Girls

Just as caddies should love golf, ball boys and girls should love tennis. And the more they know about the sport, the better their chances of getting other jobs. There are three types of tennis clubs and tournaments where you may be able to find work. Each of them requires different approaches to getting work.

Private Clubs

To get work at a private tennis club, ring up the manager and ask how to go about becoming a ball boy or girl at their club. If they're willing to give you a trial, they may give you a few tips or lessons first or they may put you straight onto the court and see how you go.

Public Courts

> 'I've been a ball girl at several major tournaments. I've handed balls to Martina Hingis, Venus Williams, Andre Agassi and Pat Rafter. It's a real buzz.'–Annette

To get work at public tennis courts, dress nicely, be polite and ask any of the players if they'd like a ball boy or ball girl for their game. The more you know about tennis, the better, because you can also offer your services as an umpire and scorer.

Professional Tournaments

To get work at a professional tennis tournament, ring the tournament organisers and ask how to apply. You'll probably be sent an official application form and must have some experience as a ball boy or ball girl or have been playing tennis for quite a while. If you do want to work at a professional tournament, contact the organisers months ahead of the tournament's date or you may miss out. Be warned, at many professional tournaments, ball boys and ball girls are not paid. They do it for the experience. However, they usually get to keep the clothes they are issued with.

Transferring Your Knowledge

N⁰ 65 Teaching Swimming

If I keep kicking really hard... in 15 years or so... I could help teach other kids to swim!

Not many part-time jobs can result in saving lives but this one can. If you believe you could teach others how to swim, then read on.

A Responsible Job

Teaching swimming is an important responsibility. Just because you can swim well doesn't mean that you will become a good teacher. Most states and countries have a minimum age limit for teachers, so check what it is where you live. It's unlikely you'll be able to teach until you turn 17. However, you can take a few steps to prepare yourself, such as attending first aid courses and finding out from your local swim centre whether there are other courses you could do.

Doing a Course

Once you turn the right age, you will have to complete a comprehensive course. This may be run by your local centre but is more likely to be run by a specialist organisation. Among the subjects the course will cover are:

• **safety in the pool** • **teaching methods** • **floating skills** • **first aid** • **dealing with the public** • **dealing with distressed children**

Quick Reactions

You will be placed in situations that will determine whether you have the capacity to become a teacher. You will need to be able to respond quickly, adapt to changing circumstances and prove that you are responsible enough to have children in your care. Once you have qualified as a teacher, there are two options open to you: teaching at a swim centre or teaching at a private venue, such as your home.

Teaching at a Pool

Almost all swim centres have learning programs for both children and adults. Therefore, they are always on the lookout for teachers. Even if they don't have a vacancy when you qualify, they may take your name and contact you if a position becomes available. If you have swum at the centre for some time and they have helped you through your courses, you have a good chance of being at the head of the queue. The main advantage of teaching at a pool is that you don't have to organise lessons. You are given your students and told when your lessons are.

Teaching Privately

Although teaching swimming in the pool at your home offers flexibility, there are a number of complications you should be aware of.

You've got to keep the water quality of the pool under control... If you let one plastic duck in the pool ... before you know it... there'll be a whole family of them living in here!

- You may have to take out special insurance to cover accidents and illness.
- You will probably have to obtain a special licence from your local council.
- You will have to buy life-saving equipment.
- Water quality must be checked constantly.
- There may be limits on the number of students you can have at any one time.
- You will have to have a change room, shower and toilet for your students.

Warning

Just because you are teaching privately, does not mean that you don't have to comply with the regulations outlined at the beginning of this section. Check with your council about the level of first aid you have to have reached and whether there is a minimum age limit for your students. Also, make sure that while you are teaching, an adult is present, keeping an eye on all the students. This adult should also have some training in first aid and rescue.

Finally, as with all jobs where you are teaching people privately, for your safety and that of your students, never be alone with a student without an adult you know present.

No **66**

Teaching Sports Skills

This is a trick I learned when I was your age. You may never need to use it... ...but hey... It sure looks SPECTACULAR!

Almost every child dreams of becoming a sports star. This is great for those who are skilled in a particular sport because it provides them with coaching work. Whatever your sport is, if you have above average ability, there are others out there who want you to help them reach the same level. Unfortunately, most of them haven't got a chance. But don't tell them that. You don't want to dishearten them or you'll do yourself out of some money.

What it Involves

Teaching a sport involves:

- improving the skill level of your students
- explaining the rules of the sport
- improving their fitness level

- giving them exercises to do on their own
- discussing the latest tactics in the sport
- showing them how to use all the equipment properly

You may also wish to teach them sportsmanship, which means the appropriate behaviour to adopt when both winning and losing.

Marketing Yourself

You obviously want to attract students who play the same sport as you. So visit all the relevant sports clubs in your area and put up notices about yourself. Include your name, phone number, sporting accomplishments and details of any training courses that you have completed. Also, introduce yourself to other trainers in your area. Offer your services as a replacement when they go on holiday or cannot coach for some other reason. If you find yourself teaching sports skills privately, make sure that an adult you know is present.

First Aid Warning

Before trying to find work as a sports trainer, you should complete a comprehensive first aid course. Injuries during sports training and practice are common. You should know exactly how to deal with concussion, sprained ankles, asthma attacks and fractured arms and legs.

My... It is a little bleeder!

With your limited knowledge of first aid... Do you think I'll live?

Special Tip...

Never neglect the basics. Every sport has certain moves and techniques that should be learnt before anything else. Stress the importance of these skills to your students and don't move onto more interesting stuff until you think they are ready, no matter how much they complain about how boring it is.

Tutoring

Can I turn on the radio and sing along while you tutor me?

Hey! You can't try that one on me! I tried that on my Mum once... ..and believe me... ..it doesn't work!

There are certain advantages in being top of the class in a particular subject. Even though your friends might tease you about being the teacher's pet, you can have the last laugh by showing them the money you're earning by transferring your knowledge to others. It doesn't matter which subject or subjects you are best at, there's always a student out there who needs your help.

Rules to Follow

Tutoring involves sitting down with a student and helping them understand a particular subject. It can be very rewarding. When the student responds positively and their grades improve, it is often the tutor who is the most pleased. The lessons may be held in the student's house, the tutor's house or somewhere else. Wherever they are held, there are certain rules you need to follow.

• Plan your lessons well. Don't turn up without having the entire lesson planned. However, you have to remain flexible enough not to get flustered if your student does not get through everything you planned.

- Make sure there are no distractions. Make sure the radio, CD player or television are turned off.
- Set some homework and make sure you mark it before the start of the next lesson.
- Encourage the student whenever possible.
- Take a short break every half hour or so. One-on-one learning can be very exhausting.
- Report back to the student's parents after each lesson. After all, they're probably the ones paying you.

Marketing Yourself

There's probably not a lot of use putting up notices at schools or where kids hang out. In most cases, it's their parents who want to hire a tutor, not the actual child. Instead, advertise in the local paper, put a notice up in your local library and even put flyers in letter boxes.

Warning

As with all jobs where you are teaching people privately, for your safety and that of your students, never be alone with a student without an adult you know present.

'I have advertised my services as a tutor a few times. The best response I ever got was near the end-of-year exams. My phone hardly stopped ringing.'
–Stephanie

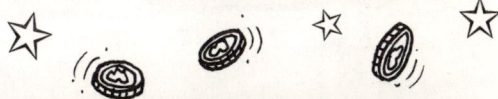

Special Tip...

There are many companies that provide tutoring services. If you don't want to have the hassle of finding your own clients, contact one of these companies and try to get on their books.

I'm just polishing up for my own Exams... But give me five minutes ...my brain will be about full...and I'll be round to tutor you for yours!

Using Your Hands

VERY BUSY HANDS

№ 68

Making Mystery Bottles

If you try and sell a handful of objects, most people would take a quick look and walk away. But put them in a fancy bottle or jar that camouflages the objects, call it a mystery bottle and suddenly people are interested.

So what's in a MYSTERY BOTTLE?

I don't know... It's a mystery!!

Maximum Appeal

Mystery bottle stalls are very popular at fetes and other public events, particularly among young children. The bottles or jars should be painted in bright colours to make them more appealing and the objects should be partially visible but not identifiable. You could even wrap the objects up in coloured paper to make the whole thing even more mysterious.

Because you are going to attract children of different ages, have a selection of bottles to suit everyone. Include:

•**things to eat (lollies or chocolate)** •**things to wear (jewellery, ribbons, watches etc)** •**things to play with (small toys)** •**things to put in a bathtub (bath salts, bath oils)** •**different bottles for boys and girls**

Special Tip...

Buy in bulk. Rather than just buying a couple of items at a time, buy as many of the same items as you can afford. If they come in a pack or box, it will almost certainly be cheaper than buying the same number one at a time. If there is no difference in price, negotiate with the store manager.

Making Electronic Gadgets

There are two types of kids: those who are good at making electronic devices and those who wish they were. The good news for those who can make electronic devices is that there is a market for their work. The good news for those who cannot make electronic devices is that there is plenty of opportunity to purchase them. So everyone's happy.

Now.... Just like in the movies... Is it the red wire I cut... or the green wire I cut to stop this thing doing whatever it does?

TICK TICK

There is virtually no end to the type of electronic devices that can be made at home. In fact, we could probably put out a book titled 101 Electronic Devices to Build at Home. If you're interested in building an electronic device, here's a good one to start with. It's relatively easy and is practical, which means you're more likely to be able to sell it.

The Super Torch (instructions provided by Paul Hauner and Luke Anderson from Newcastle, Australia)

Ask your local electronics store for:

• **one normally open push button switch**
• **one 1.2k (brown red red) resistor** • **one 10,000 mcd or up LED** • **one 9V battery** • **one 9V battery clip**
• **two lengths of red 2.5cm (1 inch) wire and two lengths of black 5cm (2 inch) wire (note: please strip all wires)**

Once you have everything:

1 Twist the red wire coming from the battery clip to the other red wire and attach the end of that lead to the leg of the resistor.

2 Twist your red lead to the long leg of the LED and the other end to the other resistor leg.

3 Twist one of your black leads to the black lead coming from the battery clip.

4 Get your other black lead and twist it to the short leg of your LED.

5 Attach both black leads to the little bits of metal coming from the switch (it doesn't matter which lead goes on which metal bit).

6 Attach the battery to the clip, press the button and the light should come on.

Warning

When working with any electronic equipment, you should be very careful. Never work with faulty wiring, always make sure that power sources are turned off until the job is complete and follow instructions exactly.

Hmmm.... Don't like the look of that smoke... Must be faulty wiring!

Nº 70
Making Greeting Cards

Holidays and celebrations can be expensive, particularly if it involves buying presents for people. This is the ideal opportunity to get into the spirit of the celebration and make some money to pay for the presents you've got to buy.

Card Tips

There are many different types of greeting cards you can make. There are also many books and web sites that give instructions on how to make them. But if you want your cards to stand out from the crowd, here are a few tips.

• Make some cards out of old cards and cardboard, then market them as recycled cards. In these days of environmental awareness, these cards will appeal to a lot of people. You can also charge a little more for these cards because they are environmentally friendly goods.

• Use materials not normally found on greeting cards, such as wool, ribbons and interesting pieces of material, such as denim.

- Use woodcuts or potato stencils to form shapes relevant to the particular celebration.
- Make cards with pop-up boxes.
- Cut your cards into shapes other than the normal rectangle.
- Make cards of all different sizes, some small enough to be used as gift tags, others large enough to stand out against other cards.
- The more work you put into your cards, the higher the price you can ask for.

Selling Your Cards

It's best to sell your cards door to door, but remain close to your street where neighbours know you. You don't want to venture into a new neighbourhood alone without an adult. If your cards are for a particular celebration, get in early. Don't wait until a couple of days before the celebration. Most people will have their cards by then.

'I get dressed up in a costume that matches the occasion when I sell my cards. Last Christmas, my friend and I dressed up as two reindeers.'—Zoe

Care to buy any of my hand drawn Easter cards?

Isn't it a little early in the year to be dressed up as Santa sonny?

Do you know how hard it is to hire a BUNNY OUTFIT this time of the year? This is all they had!

Nº 71 Making Jam/Jelly

> Just look at the stuff these kids make these days! What's this? POTATO...APRICOT and CABBAGE JAM!
>
> In my day... it was just STRAWBERRY STRAWBERRY STRAWBERRY

EXOTIC HOME MADE JAMS

Jars of jam are sold at fetes, fairs, exhibitions, shows and many other places. Sometimes it's hard to walk through a fete or fair without falling over tables of jam. So why are so many jars of jam made? Because they sell. And because they're easy to make. So what are you waiting for?

What to Use

The important thing is to use very ripe fruit. It doesn't matter if it's beginning to go a little soft, you're going to squash it anyway. If you're going to set up a stall selling jam, it's best to have a wide range. That way you're more likely to have something for everyone. There are many different fruits you can use, including:

- strawberries • raspberries • blackberries • blueberries
- plums • cherries • figs • rhubarb • apricots • peaches • quinces

and many more.

Recipe for Strawberry Jam

Ingredients:

- 2 kilograms (4.5 lb) of strawberries
- 7 cups of sugar
- 100 grams (3.5 oz) of fruit pectin (a natural thickening agent)

Marketing Tip...

Why not design a special label to make your jars stand out? A catchy design or bright colours will do the trick.

Method:

- Wash and crush strawberries.
- Mix the strawberries and sugar together in a saucepan and bring to the boil, always stirring.
- Once it has boiled, add the pectin and return to the boil.
- Keep it boiling for one minute, stirring all the time, then remove from the heat and skim any foam off the top of the mixture.
- Pour the mixture into warm, sterilised jars, seal the top and sit in a bath of boiling water for ten minutes.

Health and Safety Tip...

Always write all of your ingredients on the label. This helps people who might be allergic to something.

Nº 72

Baking Biscuits/Cookies

Hey! You're no more a Girl Guide than what I am....' And weren't you here just a while ago selling Easter cards dressed as Santa?

Yep! It's just my marketing strategy... But will you still buy my lovely cookies?

Nobody can resist freshly baked biscuits or cookies. Like jam, biscuits sell well at fairs and shows and you can even sell them door to door. After all, girl guides have been doing it for decades.

Simply Irresistible

The trick to selling biscuits is to try and sell them as soon as possible after baking them. This is when they smell and taste freshest. In fact, they're irresistible. The first few times that you bake and sell biscuits, try different types of biscuits. Once you have determined which ones sell the best, stick to making those. And remember, always write down on a sheet of paper all the ingredients you have used.

Recipe for Chocolate Biscuits

Ingredients:

- 125 grams (4.5 oz) butter
- $\frac{1}{4}$ cup castor sugar
- 1 cup self-raising flour
- pinch of salt
- $2\frac{1}{2}$ tablespoons cocoa

> "I've been making pocket money selling biscuits door to door for about two years. At first, I made a batch, then went around selling them. Now I take orders, as different people prefer different biscuits.'—Alisha

Method:

- Heat oven to 200° Celsius (390° Fahrenheit).
- Grease baking tray.
- Cream the butter until it is very soft, then slowly add the sugar, while beating the mixture. It should become white and fluffy.
- Sift the flour, salt and cocoa into a bowl, then stir it into the other mixture.
- Roll the mixture into small balls and place on baking tray.
- Flatten each ball.
- Bake for 6–8 minutes.
- Cool on wire tray.

Marketing Tip...

Give your biscuits a name that will help them sell. Don't call them chocolate biscuits, call them deep, rich, chocolate biscuits. Don't call them orange biscuits, call them extra tangy orange biscuits.

Well the SOFT and RUBBERY CREAM CARAMEL CRUMBLES sounded interesting at the time!

№ 73 Making Cakes

Don't tell me...!
Don't tell me...!
Let me guess!
It's Little Red
Riding Hood
selling
Home made
Cakes!

CAKES

RRUFF!

As with biscuits, you can sell cakes from a stall or door to door. Remember to take a note of which cakes sell the best, as well as which cake each of your customers prefers.

Taking the Taste Test

Recipes can be found in most recipe books and on numerous web sites. Always try before you sell. That means making a cake and having a taste before deciding whether it would be a good one to sell. Get your friends and family to give their opinions as well.

USING YOUR HANDS

Recipe for Banana Cake

Ingredients:

- 1 cup rice bran
- 1 cup brown sugar
- $\frac{3}{4}$ cup milk
- 2 bananas—mashed
- $\frac{1}{2}$ teaspoon cinnamon
- $1\frac{1}{2}$ cups self raising flour

Method:

- Turn oven to 180° Celsius (350° Fahrenheit).
- Mix rice bran, sugar, bananas and milk together and let sit for five minutes.
- Add flour and cinnamon and mix mixture well.
- Pour into a greased and lined loaf tin measuring 23 cm x 12 cm (9 inches x 5 inches).
- Bake for one hour (or longer if necessary).
- Cool on a wire rack.

'I try and make cakes to suit the season. I make Christmas cakes in December, heavy chocolate cakes in winter and lighter cakes in summer. I've also found out the birthdays of some of my customers and I knock on their door about a week beforehand. I've been asked to make a few birthday cakes by doing this.'–Zoe

Marketing Tip...

Put up a sign saying 10% of your profits go to a particular charity. People may be more likely to buy a cake or slice of cake if they think that some of it is going to a good cause. Make sure that you do give 10% to a charity and keep the receipts in case anyone asks. You could also put up a sign that details how much you have given to the charity through the sale of these cakes.

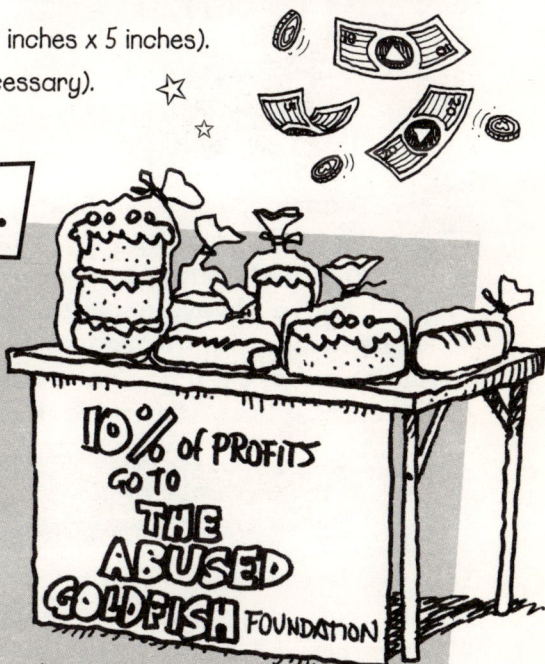

Nº 74

Drawing Caricatures/ Cartooning

Now you're going to have to use a little imagination here.... But what do you reckon...? Is it you?

A caricature is an exaggerated drawing of someone. Not everyone can draw caricatures. In fact, you probably know by now whether or not you can. If you've always expressed yourself better through drawings than words and have a constant itch to sketch people's faces, then you're ideal. If you still draw people as stick insects, then stay right away.

Getting Started

Drawing caricatures involves setting up an easel at your local shops or shopping centre and attempting to get passers-by to pay you to draw them. Before you get to this stage, you should practise by drawing your friends and family. Get honest opinions of your work. You should also consider doing a short course. Many art schools hold part-time classes in caricature drawing.

Equipment

Once you're ready to turn professional, you will need:

- **an easel** •**charcoal or pencils** •**paper**
- **a display of previous work**

Drawing the Subject

A good caricature emphasises those parts of the subject that stand out. Ask yourself the following questions:

- What shape is their face? It could be angular or round or long.
- Does the face have any lines that stand out?
- Which features of the subject's face are you drawn towards?
- Are they wearing any accessories such as glasses or jewellery?
- Is their hair all over the place or neatly brushed?

Although you want to exaggerate certain features, you must make sure not to insult your subject. The key is to concentrate on making the picture humorous but not offensive.

Marketing Tip...

Have a sign in the middle of your display offering your services for weddings. Caricatures of all wedding guests would be something many brides and grooms would treasure.

Now remember! I don't want you to draw me with a big nose! And definitely no wart on the end!

Nº 75

Making Friendship Bands

Hey... what are those things all over you?

Friendship Bands. Aren't I just the friendliest person you've ever seen!

Friendship bands are very popular items among children, particularly girls. They are given from one person to another as a mark of friendship, a sign of appreciation or as a get-well token. Although they are relatively easy to make, not everyone is going to be able to make them or could be bothered making them, so there is an opportunity for someone like you.

Instructions

There are many different types of friendship bracelets that you can make. Some have two colours, others three or more. Some are very simple, others more elaborate. Below are the instructions for a simple one.

USING YOUR HANDS

Equipment

You're going to need:

- **four different coloured embroidery threads, 66 centimetres (25 inches) long** •**a clipboard and clip** •**scissors**

Method

- Place the threads alongside each other and tie a knot about 3 cm (1 inch) from one end.
- Clip the short ends to the clipboard to make it easier to work.
- Take the thread that is furthest on the left (thread 1) and loop it over, then under the thread next to it (thread 2). Pull tight so you have created a knot.
- Repeat the move above.
- Now, loop thread 1 under and over the thread second from the right (thread 3) so that you have created another knot.
- Next, loop thread 1 under and over the thread furthest on the right (thread 4) so that you have created another knot.
- The end of thread 1 should now be on the far right, instead of the far left.
- Thread 2 is now on the extreme left. Repeat all the steps until thread 2 is on the extreme right.
- Do the same with thread 3.
- Do the same with thread 4.
- Keep going until you have the desired length. However, make sure you allow yourself an end of about 3 cm (1 inch).
- Trim the ends so that they are even.

Marketing Tip...

If you're only selling your friendship bands to girls, try making them in the colours of local football teams. It's a sure way of getting boys to buy them.

№ 76 Pressing Flowers

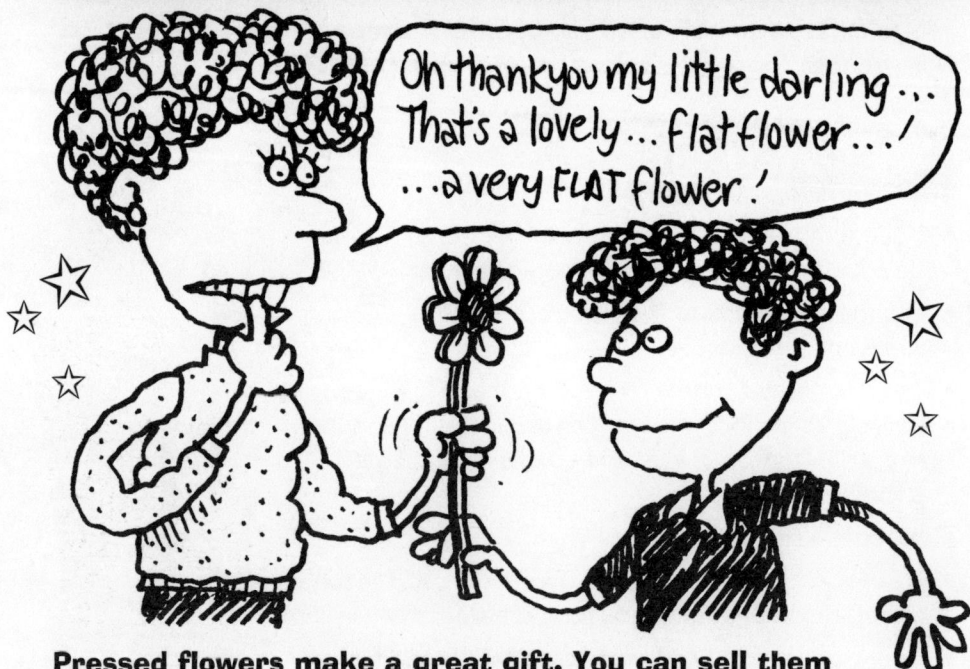

Pressed flowers make a great gift. You can sell them from a stall or directly to friends and family members. You could also give them as a present, instead of having to buy a gift. You may think that this isn't actually making money, but if it means you're not spending your own money, it has the same effect.

 Equipment

• backing board • blotting paper • craft glue • toothpicks
• newspaper • heavy books or other flat objects

 Method

• Pick the flowers, plants, leaves and grasses you want to press. Small flowers are the best to work with.

• Flatten the flowers by pressing them between your fingers.

• Place the blotting paper on top of the backing board.

USING YOUR HANDS

- Using a toothpick, apply a small amount of glue to the back of some of the flowers, plants, leaves and grasses.
- Press these flowers, plants, leaves and grasses onto the blotting paper.
- Press down with several layers of newspaper.
- Repeat the process with more flowers, plants, leaves and grasses.
- When you have the design you are after, place a piece of blotting paper on top and set the heavy books on top.
- Leave for at least 10 days.

Special Tip...

Some flowers are better than others for pressing. Among the best flowers are:

- Azaleas
- Cornflowers
- Geraniums
- Marigolds
- Buttercups
- Daffodils
- Heather
- Pansies
- Chrysanthemums
- Daisies
- Lavender
- Roses

I gotta tell you I feel really edgy sitting here Wish someone would move me!

Potting Plants

It can't be much fun being a plant. You stand up all day with your feet in manure, while someone pours water on your head. However, potting and selling plants is a great business to be in because so many people have no idea how to look after plants that they have to keep buying new ones to replace the ones they've killed. You can sell pot plants from stalls or from your garden. If selling from your garden, post flyers or put up posters in your neighbourhood.

MUM! Hey MUM! Can you find me a pot please? FAST!

This one's a BIG ONE!

POT PLANT SALE

There are three ways of potting plants for selling: digging up an entire plant from the garden and placing it in a pot; taking a cutting from a plant and cultivating that cutting; and planting seeds in a pot. Below are a few tips for each method.

Potting a Plant

- Dig right around the base of the plant.
- With one hand on top of the plant and the other under its base, gently ease the plant out of the soil.
- Make sure you have chosen a pot that is large enough to allow the new plant to grow.
- Cover the hole at the bottom of the pot with a rock or a piece of pottery.
- Cover the bottom of the pot with potting soil.
- Place the plant in the pot, then fill the pot with more potting soil.
- Water the plant.

Potting a Cutting

- Cut off the end of a plant, including a leaf or bud. The cutting should be 10–15 cm (4-6 inches) long.
- Dip the bottom of the cutting in water or in a special growth solution.
- Plant the cutting in a pot of potting soil, making sure about 80% of the cutting is beneath the soil.
- Water the cutting.

Planting Seeds

- Fill the pot with potting soil to near the top of the pot.
- Make the surface level and water the soil.
- Using a finger, make a hole for each seed. Remember, there should be enough space between the seeds to allow for growth.
- Place the seeds in the holes and cover so that the seeds are just below the surface.

Maintenance Tips...

Potting plants, cuttings and seeds is only the first step. You then have to help them grow. Here are three important tips.

- Water the plants regularly but do not overwater. You should let the soil dry between waterings.
- Do not leave plants in direct sunlight during high temperatures. A shaded area with lots of fresh air is recommended.
- Remove dead leaves or diseased areas of the plant immediately.

Safety Warning

It is recommended that you wear gloves when handling potting mix. If you do not wear gloves, make sure you wash your hands thoroughly before handling food. Some potting mix ingredients can cause illness if digested.

WOW!
I can see why it says on the side of the box to... STAND BACK WHILE FEEDING this little baby!

FREEZE DRIED WHOLE FLIES

№ 78 Making Bookmarks

In the years B.C. (Before Computers), bookmarks were something you put inside a book to mark which page you were up to. Of course now they are a function that enables you to gain quick access to certain web sites. However, traditional bookmarks are still popular.

Tell me that's not my bookmark there on the table.

Yep! That's your bookmark alright! Next you'll be asking me what page you were up to....

Types of Bookmarks

There are many different types of bookmarks you can make. Most of them are a thin, rectangular shape but there's no reason they couldn't be other shapes, so long as it pokes out from the end of the book.

Here are a few suggestions of materials that bookmarks could be made from:

•leather •cardboard •lace
•silk •velvet

And here are some special features you could include:

•photos of people or pets
•pressed flowers
•illustrations or caricatures
•special messages or greetings

Marketing Tip...

Apart from selling bookmarks at a stall or to your friends and neighbours, you could visit your local bookshop and show them a range of your work. If they like what they see, they may be willing to sell your bookmarks at their shop.

I've designed this bookmark for those with a terrible memory

That sounds like me....

What did you say its for again?

" 'Instead of designing business cards for my bookmark making business, I produced a special bookmark with my contact details. It has attracted a lot of attention.'–Tina "

№ 79

Adding Value to Olive Oil

Olive oil is used for cooking, as a salad dressing, even to dip bread into. This is a very simple idea that produces a product that looks great and is very useful.

This is my new business enterprise. Putting OLIVE OIL into bottles.

Well I think you need to go back and wash out the bottles... That one's got sticks and leaves inside it.

What You Need

• clean, clear bottles • olive oil
• special ingredients

Ingredients

The best special ingredients to use are:

• **fresh herbs, particularly rosemary and bay leaves**
• **chillies** • **slices of lemon**

Marketing Tip...

Take a few bottles into your local homeware store and show the manager or owner what great decorations they make next to products such as dinner sets and salad bowls. They may buy a few as decorative items for their store.

What to Do

• Place your special ingredients in the bottle.
• Fill with olive oil.
• Secure cap on bottle.

That's it. You've finished. It's that simple. If you want to do more, just tie a small ribbon or bow around the top of the bottle but don't decorate the bottle too much. The focus should be on the special ingredients floating in the olive oil.

Working in a Store

Nº 80

Delivering Newspapers

If you like sleeping in, don't even read this section. In most cases, delivering newspapers involves getting up very early. In fact, while it's still dark. That's because the most popular newspapers are the morning newspapers and people want to read them while they're having breakfast or on the way to work. Today, adults in cars do most newspaper deliveries, though newsagents do employ children to deliver newspapers on their bikes.

O.k Jon! Rise and shine! The sun will be up soon... Your bike is warmed up and ready to go for your paper run!

Tasks

A newspaper delivery job involves several different tasks. These include:

- rolling up and securing newspapers
- applying a waterproof cover (if there is rain about)
- checking which customers don't want their regular delivery that morning
- stacking the newspapers on their bike, in order of delivery (in some towns and cities, there are more than one daily newspaper to be delivered)
- delivering the newspapers

'I hated the early mornings at first but now that I'm used to them I don't mind at all. Delivering newspapers is a good way to earn money because the job's done before school and I have afternoons and weekends free.'—Andrew

Who to Contact

Visit your newsagent/stationery store and ask if there is a vacancy. If not, ask to be put on the waiting list. Because some people get tired of the early mornings very easily, you may make it to the top of the waiting list very quickly.

№ 81 Delivering Groceries

Fumble-fingers need not apply. If you have a habit of dropping egg cartons every time you handle them, then this job may cost you more than you earn, particularly if you have to pay for damages.

I don't recall ordering SCRAMBLED EGGS in my shopping order!

You didn't

Don't even breathe! Or that's what I'll have!

What it Involves

This job involves delivering bags or boxes of groceries from the grocery store to customers' houses. In cases where the customer lives very close to the store, you might just walk there. If they live further away and don't have too much shopping, you may be able to carry it on the front or back of your bike. For larger deliveries, you may be required to travel in a car, van or truck and deliver the groceries when the driver stops at the right address.

This is a job that requires you to be polite and friendly with customers. After all, you are a representative of the store.

Who to Contact

Ask the manager or owner of grocery stores in your neighbourhood if there is a vacancy. If not, ask to be put on the waiting list. Remember that you will probably be required to work on Saturday afternoons, as this is the day that most people do their shopping.

Special Tip...

When you deliver the groceries, ask if the customer needs help putting the groceries away. Apart from being good customer relations, you may earn a tip for your efforts.

Nº 82

Odd Jobs at Hairdressing Salons

Although it takes a long time to learn how to cut hair properly, there are many other jobs that can be done in a hairdressing salon by untrained people. And if you are interested in a career as a hairdresser, it's a great way to learn what the job involves.

I'm keen to impress... seeing I'm only helping out.

Three times the normal amount of shampoo should clean your hair three times as well I figure.

Tasks

So what might you be asked to do if you get a job in a hairdressing salon? Well, at least some of the following:

•sweeping the floor •making tea and coffee •sterilising the equipment •washing customers' hair •taking payment and giving change •arranging products on display

Who to Contact

Ask the manager or owner of salons in your neighbourhood if there is a vacancy. If not, ask to be put on the waiting list. Remember that you will probably be required to work on Saturdays, as this is the most popular day for hair cuts.

> 'I've been a professional hairdresser for three years. I started in the business as a part-time helper. Then I became an apprentice and finally a qualified hairdresser.'–Sophie

№ 83 Stacking Shelves

Have you ever wondered why supermarket shelves are always full, even though customers are constantly taking items from them and you never see anyone replacing the stock? Well, the answer is that when the store is closed (or late at night in 24-hour supermarkets), a special breed of workers appear. They are the shelf stackers.

There are people in the supermarket who work the cash registers ...there are people who pack the bags...

I guess with those legs... this is the guy who stacks those really tall shelves!

What They Do

Shelf stackers make sure that:

- the shelves are full
- products are in the right place
- products are marked with the right price (sometimes this involves using a barcode scanner)
- empty boxes are put in the rubbish dump

Shelf stackers should be known as 'the invisible people' because the customers and other employees rarely see them.

Special Tip...

Employees at some supermarkets and grocery stores receive a discount on goods they buy. As a result, your family could save a lot of money on their grocery bill if you work as a shelf stacker.

Who to Contact

Ask the manager or owner of grocery stores and supermarkets if there is a vacancy. If not, ask to be put on the waiting list. Remember that this job usually involves evening, night and even early morning work.

№ 84

Picking up Trolleys

Supermarket trolleys can end up in lanes, front gardens, even in rivers. Fortunately, most trolleys are just abandoned in supermarket car parks. Supermarkets hire people to pick these trolleys up for three main reasons.

*I just woke up this morning...
...and there it was.
Dumped in my daisies at the bottom of my garden one of your shopping trolleys!*

Could you send someone down to push it back to your store please.'

1 They are a hazard to cars in the car park.
2 They could be damaged and they are costly to repair or replace.
3 If they are left until the end of the day, the supermarket might run out of trolleys for its customers.

Strength and Skill

Although picking up trolleys may seem to be an easy job, it does require strength and skill. Pushing trolleys back to the supermarket one at a time takes too long, so a number of trolleys are pushed inside one another and then pushed to the supermarket together. This requires a great deal of strength. You also have to be very careful not to let them get out of control, particularly when pushing them downhill, because they could run into parked or moving cars.

Who to Contact

Ask the manager or owner of grocery stores and supermarkets if there is a vacancy. If not, ask to be put on the waiting list.

'The best part of my job is what I call 'the trolley hunt'. My boss and I drive around the neighbourhood, looking for trolleys that have been taken home or dumped. We once spotted one that had been put half way up a tree.' – Tony

Nº 85

Carrying Shopping to Cars

Lots of kids hang around shopping centres. Here's a way you can earn money while hanging around shopping centres.

I was only just saying I needed another four arms to carry these bags... when you just appeared out of nowhere...

Things to Remember

That's our job..! To carry bags that is... Not to appear out of nowhere

Look out for people with a lot of shopping and offer to carry it to their car for them. Elderly people and mothers with children are particularly good opportunities. However, before you take up this idea, there are several things you should remember:

• Always ask permission from the store manager or security manager. If they say no, don't take it personally. It's probably because they don't want their customers being hassled. And don't ignore them if they say no. You'll end up in trouble.

• Look presentable and be polite. Being approached outside a shop can be confronting. You want to put potential customers at ease. As you approach, smile and say, 'Hi, I'm [your name]. Would you like some help carrying your shopping to your car?'

• Don't ask for money. Although this is what you're doing it for, if you don't ask for money, it will appear as if you're just a nice guy. You'll probably end up being offered a larger tip than the amount you would have asked for.

• If you're not offered money, remain polite. There's always next time.

You could also ask a store manager if you can offer this service on behalf of the store. Instead of being paid by the customers, you would be paid by the store.

Nº 86

Walking People to their Cars with an Umbrella

I waited for a rainy day to start my business... But I guess it's raining so hard that nobody's come out shopping!

This is a job for rainy days. You'd look pretty silly offering to keep people dry on sunny days. The same rules apply as in the 'Carrying Shopping to Cars' section.

Again, you can operate independently of the store or centre (with their permission) or as part of a store's personal service. Some store managers may need convincing that it is a good idea but if you turn up every time it rains, they're bound to give in and give you a go some time.

Special Note

If the shopping centre only has an underground car park, forget this idea.

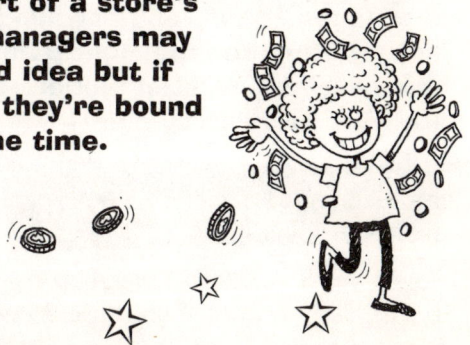

No.

87

Sign-writing at Christmas and other Holidays

This is the ultimate in public art, though it's probably not a good idea to add your tag to the finished product. Small shops often want to join in with the Christmas spirit but do not have enough spare people to do the work required or enough money to pay a professional sign-writer.

What it Involves

Sign-writing involves painting special designs and messages on shop windows. At Christmas time, the designs could be of Santa, reindeers or a nativity scene, while the messages could include 'Seasons Greetings' and 'We Wish You a Merry Christmas'. At other times during the year, they may want messages about a special sale.

Equipment

To do this job, you're going to need:

•**stencils of the designs and messages** •**paint (ask at your paint supply store for the right paint to use on glass)** •**a step ladder** •**a rag (to wipe away stray paint)**

Special Tip...

While you're talking to the store owner or manager about painting their windows for Christmas, also ask whether they'd like you to put their decorations up. They can only say no.

Getting Work

To get work, walk into every shop in your neighbourhood and ask if you can paint their windows. If you have done a few before, take photos of your work so they know that you can do the job.

Getting Your Hands Dirty
(The jobs nobody wants to do)

Nº 88

Ironing

Why do so many people walk around in crumpled clothes? It's because they hate ironing. Ironing is one of the most unpopular household chores and people go to extraordinary efforts to avoid ironing.

Ironing Tips

Before setting up an ironing business, you should have a lot of practice. Offer to iron your family's clothes for a couple of weeks. If you're not willing to do that, you haven't got the commitment to this sort of work. When ironing, remember the following tips:

- Always read the instructions on each item. They will tell you what material the garment is made from and may give specific ironing instructions.

- Synthetics and silks should be ironed at a low to medium temperature.

- Woollen items should be ironed at a medium to high temperature.

- Cottons and linens should be ironed at a high temperature.

- Do not iron in a circular motion as this can stretch the garment.

- Always keep the iron moving. This avoids unseemly marks.

- When ironing a shirt, start with the collar, then the shoulder, followed by the cuffs, the sleeves and the body. Finish by repressing the collar.

- When ironing trousers, pull the pockets out and iron them first. Then, iron the waist, followed by each leg in turn.

- Linen items should be dampened slightly before being ironed.

- Always hang up the items immediately after they've been ironed.

How to Charge

You can charge per hour or per item.
If you work out a fair rate per item, your client knows exactly how much they're going to pay before you start.

Safety Warning

Ironing can be dangerous. Always follow these rules:

- Never, ever touch the plate of the iron. If you want to test whether the iron is on, sprinkle some water onto the plate and see if it sizzles.

- If you are going to stop ironing for even a short period, turn the iron off. If you leave the iron on and it topples over, it could start a fire.

- Be careful not to tangle the cord while you're ironing. If you trip over the tangled cord, the hot iron could fall onto you.

AHHRR... JUST RIGHT!

Special Tip...

If you're operating an ironing business from your home, offer a free pick-up and delivery service to your customers.

Nº89 Polishing Silverware

Every now and again, adults put on a fancy dinner party. It's usually when they want to impress someone, like a boss or some new friends. Or it's for a special occasion, such as a birthday, anniversary or Christmas. To make the occasion extra special, they bring out their best crockery and cutlery. For some people, this means silver or silver plated knives, forks and spoons.

I'm the Genie of the antique silver teapot. You've scored three wishes of your choice!

Great! You can start with polishing all that lot over there

And while your doing that... I'll think about the other two wishes

What it Involves

Polishing silverware is not a difficult job, it's just tedious. With so many pieces in a dinner set, it takes a long time to clean everything. That's why people don't like it. But it's a job that has to be done because silverware tarnishes. This occurs because silver tarnishes when it comes in contact with air. To polish silverware, you just rub hard, rinse and dry.

Equipment

To polish silverware, you will require the following equipment:

• silver polish or spray • a polishing cloth
• a basin or sink of warm water • a tea towel • a polishing cloth • white gloves

Steps to Take

The polish or spray that you use will probably have instructions. You could also do the following:

1 Apply polish to the piece of cutlery and rub firmly until the tarnish and discolour disappears.
2 Rinse the cutlery thoroughly in the warm water.
3 Dry each piece of cutlery with the tea towel.
4 Put on the clean, white gloves. This is to stop you getting fingerprints all over the clean cutlery.
5 Give each piece of cutlery a final polish with the polishing cloth (but no polish).

Marketing Tip...

- While you're polishing someone's silver cutlery set, look around and see what other silverware items they have. Offer to clean them as well (for a small extra fee, of course).

I'm offering a half price deal this month on polishing silver egg cups... Can I interest you in polishing your grubby set?

- As Christmas approaches, ask all your relatives and friends whether they are going to host a big Christmas gathering. If so, suggest they use their best silver cutlery set (if they have one), which you'll polish for them.

Warning

As with all jobs, if you are going to be working in someone's house, only do so if they are a friend, family member, have been recommended by a friend or family member, or you are accompanied by an adult you know well.

No 90

Picking up Doggie Do

This job can be tackled two ways. Gloves need to be worn with both.

Come on.... Do that DO little doggy! It's worth it's weight in cash to me!

Method One

Method one involves contacting every dog owner that you know and offering to regularly clean their garden of the doggie do. Payment could be a fixed rate each time you come or dependent on the amount that you collect.

This guy is making me so nervous I can't go

Method Two

Method two involves contacting everyone in a particular street and offering to regularly clear the street of doggie do. Each householder who agrees would pay you a small fee. You could charge dog owners a higher fee as their pets are probably largely responsible for the mess.

GETTING YOUR HANDS DIRTY

Equipment

For this job, you will need:

•gloves •a scooper •a bag •a peg (to stick on your nose)

Disposal

The doggie do that you pick up can be disposed of by placing the bag/s that you have collected in the regular garbage, or by burying the doggie do in your garden bed or putting it on the compost heap and then throwing the bags away in the regular garbage.

Warning

As with all jobs, if you are going to be working in someone's house or garden, only do so if they are a friend, family member, have been recommended by a friend or family member, or you are accompanied by an adult you know well.

Safety Warning

If you are asked to clean up the mess in someone's garden, ask that they tie the dog up while you work. Dogs can get very protective of their environment and may attack someone they don't recognise.

WHACK!!!

№ 91

Washing Windows

These windows have nothing to do with computers. They're the kind that you look through. Your job is to clean them so they sparkle. Most homes and businesses have so many windows that the thought of cleaning them can be daunting. So when you come along with a bucket and sponge, you'll be welcomed with open arms.

If I could clean every window in this building... I could retire before I finish school!

Equipment

To wash windows, you're going to need:

•cleaning solution •two buckets •cloths •a squeegee on a pole •paper towels, newspaper or a chamois •a ladder

Method

Here's the simplest way to wash windows that you can easily reach.

• Drop the cloth in a bucket containing the cleaning solution.

• Wring the cloth out, then wash the window.

• Dry the window clean with paper towels, newspaper or a chamois.

For those you can't reach:

- Dip the squeegee in a bucket containing the cleaning solution.
- Clean the window with the squeegee, moving the squeegee from top to bottom, not side to side.
- Dip the squeegee in a bucket with clean water.
- Apply the squeegee to the window again, this time to rinse it.
- In between strokes, wipe the end of the squeegee with a paper towel.

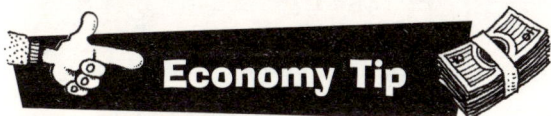

Economy Tip

If you want to save a little money, make up your own cleaning solution. Mix four tablespoons of ammonia or vinegar to one litre (one quart) of water. Never mix both ammonia and vinegar in the same solution.

Safety Tip

If you cannot reach windows by using the squeegee on a pole, leave them. Do not start climbing up ladders. It is too dangerous. Professional window cleaners have to take precautions and use a harness. Explain to your customers before you start that very high windows will have to go unwashed. They'll understand. They'd rather have an unwashed window than an injured person to deal with.

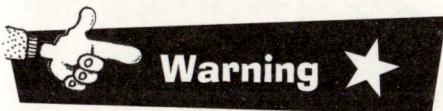

Warning

As with all jobs, if you are going to be working in someone's house or garden, only do so if they are a friend, family member, have been recommended by a friend or family member, or you are accompanied by an adult you know well.

Cleaning Out Gutters

This is a job that will take you straight to the top of someone's house, while leaving your feet firmly on the ground. It involves using a specially made device to clear leaves, twigs and mud out of the gutters around a house and then making sure the guttering system is not blocked. Your most likely customers are elderly people who cannot climb up ladders any more.

Hmmmm.... Perhaps my latest creation the... "GUTTER-CLEANER-OUTER" works a little too well! It's back to the workshop for some fine tuning.

Equipment

To clean gutters properly you will need:

• a cleaning device (instructions below) • a garbage bag • rubber gloves • a hose

Making the Cleaning Device

Find a long pole and attach a scraping device to the end, using strong twine. The head of a hand trowel is suitable, or you can make one yourself. Also attach a mirror that is large enough for you to see from the ground but small enough not to get in the way. You are going to have to position the mirror so that you can see what is in the gutter and whether or not you are scraping everything up. The only way to do this is to set it in one position and check it out. Keep altering the position until it is exactly right.

Method

- Using the mirror on the cleaning device, check out where the rubbish is.

- By moving the pole along the gutter, scrape the rubbish out of the gutter and onto the ground. Be careful not to get the scraping device caught on the edge of the gutter. You don't want to bring the whole guttering system down.

- Once you have cleared all the rubbish out of the gutter, pick it up (wearing your gloves) and put it in the garbage bag.

- Using a hose, spray some water in the gutter and see if it flows out. This is to make sure there are no blockages. If the water does not flow out properly, tell the owner.

- Once you have checked that there are no blockages, spray some water right along the gutters to rinse them clean.

- Take the garbage bag home and put the dirt in your garden or compost bin and dispose of the garbage bag in the regular garbage collection.

'I ring all of my customers in spring and autumn (fall) and remind them that it's time for their gutters to be checked. Most thank me for reminding me and ask me to come along.' –Mike

Nº 93

Removing Spiders and Bugs

Have your freedom my prickly legged little bug... may you find a new home in somebody elses yard.

WOH! What a lucky break! It could have been the BUG SPRAY for me!

This is where we find out whether you're an animal liberationist or not. There are two ways of getting rid of spiders and bugs—carefully removing them and letting them go, or killing them

Letting Your Neighbours Know

There are many people who are scared of spiders and bugs. You may be one of them, in which case this job may not be very suitable for you. If you let neighbours know that you're available to get rid of spiders and bugs in their house, you may find yourself being called on regularly. But be warned, you might get a phone call at 3:00 in the morning.

Removing Spiders and Bugs

For those who care about all living creatures, the best way to remove spiders and bugs is by catching them in a cup or glass. To do this:

- locate the spider/bug
- slam the open end of the cup/glass over the spider/bug
- lift one side of the cup/glass just enough to slip a piece of paper or thin piece of cardboard over the entire opening of the cup/glass
- tip the cup/glass the right way up, keeping one hand firmly on the paper or cardboard
- take the cup/glass a long way from the house, place it on the ground and remove the paper or cardboard

Killing Spiders and Bugs

For those who do not care about all living creatures, follow these steps:

- **locate the spider/bug** • **spray it with insecticide or**
- **squash it with a swatter or other object or** • **vacuum it**

Safety Tips

- Before you start, become very familiar with the types of spiders and bugs that live in your area. Your local library or council should be able to help you out. If you recognise a spider as being dangerous, do not attempt to remove it or kill it. Phone your local council immediately for advice.

- Always wear thick gloves. Gardening gloves are good. A spider or bug bite is unlikely to penetrate such gloves.

- If you are bitten, ring your local hospital immediately. You should carry their phone number with you at all times. Give them a description of the spider or bug and follow their instructions.

When Mum offered me her gardening gloves for this job... at first I laughed... But after seeing the bite on this little critter ... without the gloves... I'd be in a spot of bother! ...Thanks Mum!

№ 94

Taking Out the Garbage

If you've always wanted to work at the rubbish tip, here's the way to start your career. All you have to do is offer to take out the garbage for your neighbours on garbage night and return the emptied bin to its place the next day. Your most likely customers will be elderly people who are unable to wheel or carry a large garbage bin to the side of the street.

One day... maybe one day I can drive the trucks that collect these things...'

Being Environmentally Aware

In the past, this job would have required you to take just one bin out. These days, with people more environmentally aware, you'll probably have to take out a garbage bin, a bottle bin and a pile of newspapers and cardboard. Make sure that the newspapers and cardboard are well secured, so that they do not fly away before being collected.

Special Tip...

Before a major holiday period, contact your neighbours and offer to take their garbage bin in and out if they are going away. Although there may not be anything in the bin, it acts as a deterrent to home invaders. A bin not put out in the holiday season is a sure sign that someone is away.

№ 95

Weeding

There are many stories about well-meaning gardeners pulling out rare plants in the belief that they were weeds. So the first piece of advice to anyone thinking about weeding is to do your homework. Even if you think you know what you're doing, ask the owner to point out what they want removed. This will avoid unpleasant incidents.

This weed looked like a nasty piece of work... so I ripped it out quick smart before it spread!

WEED!! That's not a WEED!! That's my near extinct Montezuma's Temple of the Sun Hybrid Tiger Lily from the Andes!!

Weeding Tips

- When you're pulling out a weed, make sure you pull out the whole weed, including the root.
- Wetting the ground before you weed will make it easier to pull weeds out because it will loosen their root system.
- Hoe the ground in between flowers and plants as it will disturb young weeds before they take root.
- If weeds are growing between paving stones or bricks, pour boiling water on them.

Safety Tips

- Weeding can be hard on the back. Make sure that you regularly stand and stretch. Also, have a towel handy for you to kneel on. That way stones and other materials won't dig directly into your knees.
- Always wear gloves.

Animals

Nº 96

Walking Dogs

Get fit and earn money at the same time. Walking dogs can be fun, but you have to be alert. Dogs have a habit of trying to get their own way.

I said... RUN ROVER... RUN! So that's exactly what he did. He's such an obedient dog!

SIT ROVER?...SIT!

Tips

- Ask the owner for instructions, such as the length of the walk, the route to take and whether the dog has any peculiarities. Always follow these instructions.
- If you walk a dog at a particular time, make sure you turn up. Once dogs are in the habit of being walked at a particular time, they expect it.
- Let the dog walk at its pace. Don't rush it. If it wants to stop and sniff, let it.
- Keep your dog away from other dogs.
- Take a bag and pooper scooper to clean up mess left by your dog. (You didn't think you were just going to earn money by having a walk, did you?)
- Keep your dog on a lead while on the pavement. If you go to a park, read any signs to see if there are restrictions on exercising dogs there.
- You can walk two dogs at a time only if they have the same owner. Otherwise, they might not get on and you'll have your hands full controlling them.

Special Tip...

If you have a dog who loves going fast and you have problems keeping up, wear a pair of inline skates. Then hold onto the leash, let the dog go for it and enjoy the ride. Also, make sure you wear protective gear such as a helmet, knee and elbow pads.

Marketing Tip...

To get business, keep an eye out for dogs in the neighbourhood. Drop a flyer in their owner's letterbox or approach the owner while they're walking the dog. And if someone wants you to walk more than one dog at a time, charge a higher price.

Nº 97

Minding Pets

Pet owners have three options when they go on holidays. They can take their pet with them, although it limits the places they can go to; they can board their pet at a veterinarian or special boarding clinic; or they can leave their pet at home and have someone look after it. In most cases they would prefer to leave their pet at home but they don't always know someone reliable who will look after it.

I don't know exactly what REX is... But the neighbour said..."Feed him with a stick...and definitely don't take him for a walk!"

REX

GGRRR RRR RRR RR R

Responsibility

Minding someone's pet while they are away is a big responsibility. It is not just a matter of putting a bit of food and water out once or twice a day. Unless the pet is a fish in a bowl, you are going to have to visit the pet in its own home. Most pets do not react well to being in another house.

Tips

Here are a few tips if you are considering minding pets.

• Find out what it eats, how much it eats and when it eats. Follow the owner's instructions exactly, even if the pet appears to want more.

• Find out what sort of exercise it does and how often it should be exercised. Make sure you give the pet all the exercise you are supposed to.

• Find out about its toilet habits. If a pet's toilet habits change, it could be a sign that something is wrong with the pet.

ANIMALS

- Find out whether the pet is allowed inside or outside the house. Don't change the pet's routine or you could cause the pet to develop bad habits.
- Find out if the pet requires medication. If it does, make sure you give the correct doses at the right times.
- Find out about the pet's playing habits. Does it have favourite toys and favourite games?
- Get the details of the pet's vet. Keep the phone number handy and ring the vet if you are at all worried about the pet's behaviour.
- Get the details of where the pet's owners are staying. If something serious happens, ring them and let them know.

Marketing Tip...

Offer your customers extra services. Seeing as you're going to be looking after their pets, you could also water their plants, bring in their mail, open and shut their blinds at the start and finish of the day and do various other jobs that will make it look as though the house is occupied.

Special Tip...

Always spend a bit of time with the pet before the owners go away. Pets can sometimes take a dislike to people and if this happens it's better for all parties if the owners hire someone else.

While you were away on holidays I was going to water your plants... but Spot did that... and bring in your mail... but as you can see... he did that too!

'I minded Cassie, a Dalmatian, when its owner had to go away for work. Cassie and I got on so well that now, two years later, I get paid to exercise Cassie three times a week.'–Georgia

№ 98

Washing Pets

Some animals love having baths. Others hate it. Unfortunately, sometimes you don't know how they're going to react until you try to get them in water. So be prepared. Unless you know someone with a pet monkey, you'll probably only be asked to wash a dog or a cat. And even then, you'll wash far fewer cats than dogs because cats basically lick themselves clean.

I'll lick myself clean ...I'll lick myself clean!

Equipment

To set up a pet wash business you will need:

•a bathtub •a rubber mat •a hair brush and/or comb •a bucket or hose •cotton balls •pet shampoo •mineral oil •cloths •towels •a hair dryer •flea powder

Washing a Dog

- Place the rubber mat in the bath so that the dog does not slip.
- Pour some warm water into the bathtub.
- Put a few drops of mineral oil into the dog's eyes. This will protect their eyes from the shampoo.
- Place cotton balls in the dog's ears to protect the ears from water.
- Brush all tangles out of the dog's coat.
- Using the bucket or hose, wet the dog all over.
- Apply the shampoo and lather thoroughly.
- Rinse the shampoo off, then wash the dog's face with a cloth that has no soap on it.

- Get the dog out of the bathtub and dry with towels.
- Turn the hair dryer on and apply air to the dog, keeping hair dryer at least 15 centimetres (6 inches) from the coat.

Washing a Cat

- Place the rubber mat in the bath so that the cat does not slip.
- Put a few drops of mineral oil into the cat's eyes. This will protect its eyes from the shampoo.
- Place cotton balls in the cat's ears to protect the ears from water.
- Brush all tangles out of the cat's coat.
- Pour some warm water over the cat.
- Apply the shampoo and lather thoroughly.
- Rinse the shampoo off, then wash the cat's face with a cloth that has no soap on it.
- Dry the cat with towels.
- Turn the hair dryer on and apply air to the cat, keeping hair dryer at least 15 centimetres (6 inches) from the coat.

Marketing Tip...

Be especially keen to get customers who have white dogs or cats. Dirt shows up much easier on white pets and you'll probably have to wash them more regularly than dark coloured pets.

It's O.K... I'm just as grubby as you... you just can't see the grime on me..'

'I went to a customer's house to wash their dog. While I was there I noticed they had three guinea pigs. I offered to wash the guinea pigs for a dollar each and the owner agreed.'–Jeff

Nº 99

Cleaning Kennels and Cages

Boy...! For a little bird... you make a mighty big mess!

Pet animals can be cute, adorable and very lovable. They can also make a great mess. Kennels and cages can get very messy and smelly and need cleaning regularly. This job is particularly good for kids thinking of becoming veterinarians when they leave school. It gives them some experience of what's involved in looking after animals.

Where to Find Work

There are four main places where you can find work cleaning kennels and cages.

• First, you can ask friends or relatives who own pets whether you can go to their house and clean the pet's cage or kennel. Remember never to go to the house of someone you don't know without an adult present.

- Second, you can ask your local veterinarian if they need someone to clean out cages and kennels. Some veterinarians keep sick pets overnight or board pets while their owners are on holiday.
- Third, you can ask at a pet boarding facility, if there is one nearby.
- Fourth, you can ask at an animal shelter or lost animals home, if there is one nearby.

What it Involves

The way that you do your job depends on whether you have to remove the pet from the cage or kennel or whether you can do the cleaning with the pet inside the cage or kennel. Basically, you need to:

- empty food and water bowls or containers and fill with fresh food and water
- sweep or wipe out all dirt and waste
- remove dirty newspaper, shavings or other floor covering and replace with fresh newspaper, shavings or other floor covering
- wipe the sides and top of the cage or kennel
- check that there are no sharp edges appearing
- dispose of all the rubbish you have collected

Removing Pets from Cages and Kennels

If a pet has to be removed before you start cleaning its cage or kennel, get the owner of the pet or the owner of the facility to remove the pet and put it somewhere safe. They will have more experience and know the pet's personality and habits better than you. If you do have to remove the pet yourself, make sure that you have discussed its behaviour with the owner of the pet or the owner of the facility.

While you are removing the pet, concentrate very hard on what you are doing. Do not take your eyes off the pet. Wear thick gloves and long sleeves to protect you from bites and scratches.

If the pet begins to struggle and looks likely to attack you, back away and leave the cage alone. It is not worth being bitten just to clean their cage.

Once the pet has been removed, it may have to be put in a safe place, while you are busy cleaning. You don't want it escaping. This means having another cage nearby, especially for mice, birds, rabbits and guinea pigs.

Cleaning with a Pet in the Cage

If you are cleaning a cage or kennel while the animal remains inside, always be aware of where the animal is. Make soothing noises the whole time to reassure the animal. If it's possible to wear thick gloves while working, do so. They will offer some protection against scratches and bites. It's also a good idea to have a rolled-up newspaper nearby. That way you can wave it at the animal or, as a last resort, hit the animal with it if the animal approaches aggressively.

Safety Warning

If an animal scratches or bites you, immediately seek treatment from a doctor or at a hospital. If possible, share this job with a friend, with one of you doing the cleaning and the other watching or holding the animal.

Now... Patch the dog definitely was out playing happily in the backyard... wasn't he?

Then.... Maybe he was still in his dog house

WOOFFFFF

PATCH

Nº 100

Personalising and Decorating Pet Accessories

Here's an idea that suits those who love animals and who have the creative touch. Does that sound like you? There are so many types of pet accessories that you can personalise or decorate. And you can sell your products from a stall or door to door.

Does Ginger like the spotty rug with the lace trim then for his basket?

Doesn't she know I can't stand lace ... and I don't sleep on anything spotty

What You Can Do

There are many ways that you can personalise or decorate pet accessories. You can:

- paint or stencil patterns or names on bowls
- add embroidery features to coats
- add decorations such as pom poms to baskets
- engrave initials in collars

Think how many pet accessories there are:

•**bowls** •**collars** •**rugs** •**coats** •**boots** •**hats** •**kennels** •**baskets** •**pouches that owners can wear to carry small pets on a walk**

Marketing Tip...

If you know a pet's name, paint or embroider the pet's name on an accessory. Then, take the accessory to the owner's house and tell them that the pet rang up and ordered the accessory itself. The owner will probably be so amused that they'll buy the accessory from you.

BUSTER ... What's this I hear about you ordering products over the phone with my credit card? Is it true?

Now let your imagination go wild. Purchase a cheap, ordinary looking pet accessory (or make one yourself), then decorate it to look attractive. In the business world, this is called adding value. That's exactly what you are doing: adding value to an ordinary product. And once you've done so, you can sell it for a lot more than you bought it for.

Nº 101

★ Collecting and Selling Eggs ★

Here's another idea for those who live on farms or who keep chickens, geese or ducks. The best place to sell home-grown eggs is from a roadside stall. Have a large sign and use words that will attract attention such as 'Farm Fresh Eggs', 'Home Grown Eggs' and 'Nature's Pride Eggs'.

Think of one of these little beauties as a carton of eggs in one big shell!

And believe me ...if you drop it... it makes just as much mess as a whole carton of eggs...!

VERY LARGE FARM EGGS

Peak Condition

Collecting, handling and packing eggs is not just a matter of picking them up and putting them in a container. There are several things you can do to make sure your eggs are in the best possible condition at the time of selling.

- Fresh eggs are the best eggs. Check for eggs at least twice a day, with your first check in the morning. That way they won't have time to get broken or lose some of their nutritional value.

- Collect eggs in a clean container so that the eggs are not stained by dirt or other materials.

- Wash eggs with warm water as soon as you have collected them. However, do not sit the eggs in water.

- Dry and cool the eggs immediately after washing.

- Store eggs in egg cartons with the small ends facing down.

Marketing Tip...

Contact an egg carton manufacturer and buy cartons that have no names or markings on them. Then, you can print your contact details on the cartons and perhaps a catchy name for your eggs.

"'I put a copy of a recipe requiring eggs in each carton I sell. It doesn't cost any extra and it makes people remember me.'—Lindy"

INDEX

Index

INDEX